KU-485-610

David Jacobs' BOOK OF CELEBRITIES' JOKES & ANECDOTES

Edited by Ella Glazer

compiled with the
CELEBRITIES GUILD OF GREAT BRITAIN

Illustrations by Steven Nemethy

Robson Books

THIS PAPERBACK EDITION FIRST PUBLISHED IN GREAT BRITAIN IN 1980 BY
ROBSON BOOKS LTD., 28 POLAND STREET, LONDON W1V 3DB. ORIGINALLY
PUBLISHED IN HARDBACK BY ROBSON BOOKS IN 1979. COPYRIGHT © 1979
THE CELEBRITIES GUILD OF GREAT BRITAIN

British Library Cataloguing in Publication Data.
David Jacobs Book of Celebrities, Jokes and Anecdotes.

1. English Wit and Humour

1. Glazer, Ella

2. Celebrities Guild of Great Britain

827'.9'1408 PN6175

ISBN 0-86051-087-5 HB
ISBN 0-86051-125-1 PB

The anecdotes in this book were
generously donated by our
famous contributors to the
CELEBRITIES GUILD OF GREAT BRITAIN,
to whose fund-raising
efforts all royalties will be given.

All rights reserved. No part of this publication may
be reproduced, stored in a retrieval system, or
transmitted in any form or by any means,
electronic, mechanical, photocopying, or
otherwise, without the prior permission in writing
of the publishers.

Printed in Great Britain by
Biddles Ltd, Guildford, Surrey

Preface

Noblesse Oblige became the motto of the CELEBRITIES GUILD OF GREAT BRITAIN from the moment it was founded.

None could be more apt. And one of its first distinguished Patrons was David Jacobs, indefatigable worker for charity. As busy at fund-raising gala dinners, bazaars, quizzes and panels as he is in his own right as a broadcaster, author and entertainer second-to-none, to the CELEBRITIES GUILD he has been an active Patron and reliable friend since its inception.

In a way, this book is a tribute to him and his friends—its contributors and the charitable work they do. They have rallied to our appeal to help a worthy cause—many of them not for the first time—and we are enormously indebted to them all. But it is also a tribute to the work of the CELEBRITIES GUILD, and the support it so gratefully receives.

Now comprising more than 300 prominent people, the CELEBRITIES GUILD raises funds wherever and whenever it can with all sorts of pleasurable events throughout the year.

As Founder and Chairman, I personally have had the

satisfaction of seeing money come in to provide deaf children with hearing aids, to help the research for Multiple Sclerosis, to give refugees a new start in a new land, and this year, look forward to providing financial aid to gifted children whose talents otherwise could not be fostered, and towards building a unit for adolescent autistic children.

With the help of other illustrious Patrons equally as kind and generous as David Jacobs, with my distinguished, warm-hearted co-chairman, Harold Berens, with the advice of Council members, and with a hard-working Committee, we have accumulated the friendship and encouragement of Celebrities all over the world who tirelessly produce pleasure for the public at our request. This book is one such project, and to every one of them it is a token of our deep appreciation.

So, although the GUILD has had its serious aspect, it is because *Noblesse Oblige* that it gives pleasure; we do hope you will think this is what our book has achieved.

Ella Glazer.

Ella Glazer, Chairman

Introduction

When this collection of stories was suggested, I was the one detailed to collect them. It seemed a rather daunting task at first, but once I got into my stride, and the anecdotes came rolling in, I began to enjoy the task more and more, just as I hope you will enjoy this book.

It is for your pleasure and at the same time to raise funds for the less fortunate among us. I should point out that one or two of the jokes are by no means new, because I actually asked for people's favourites; so you may well have heard some of them before.

Here's mine for starters . . .

Juke Box Jury was on our screens first time around, once a week non-stop for eight-and-a-half years and, not only did I introduce that and an afternoon programme called *Wednesday Magazine*, I was also to be seen on *A Song For Europe*, *The Ivor Novello Awards*, *Come Dancing*, *Miss World*, *The Frank Sinatra Show* – you name them, I was probably on them. So, not unnaturally, I had at that time probably one of the most recognisable faces in the country.

On a rare, hot summer's day, I was driving to Sussex when I had a craving for a long, cool glass of milk (the face of Zoe Newton, the milk girl, always did appeal to me).

I stopped at one of those delightfully welcoming road-side cafés, so much a feature of our rural life, and, just as I got to the door, it was being locked by an extremely ugly girl. When I waved at her through the steamed-up glass, she unlocked it and asked me what I wanted. I told her. She turned round and called out to her father, the proprietor:

"Oy, Dad, it's the man from the telly"

"You tell him to **** off; I've paid the instalments!"

"No, not *that* telly man" she replied. "The Juke Box man".

"I told you before", he shouted, "I'm not having one of those bleeding noisy things in here!"

It just remains for me to thank all those who contributed, and to wish you a happy time in their company.

David Jacobs

LARRY ADLER

Here's two nice ones to start off with – both short . . .

Golda Meir, in Moscow on her 70th birthday.

Brezhnev says, "Golda, baby, it's your birthday. Anything you want, you name it, it's yours."

Golda says, "Okay, tell you what. For one day, open

the borders of the USSR. Anybody wants to leave, they leave. Everybody else stays."

Brezhnev: "Golda, you little devil, you want to be *alone with me!*"

★   ★   ★

Rabbi, in synagogue, praying.

Rabbi: "God, none but you can help me in my terrible predicament. My only son is about to turn Christian."

God: "*Your* son."

9

KINGSLEY AMIS

The Van Der Merwe stories originated in South Africa, but now they are known all over the world. Van Der Merwe is the archetypal booby and blockhead – the man who uses a kind of insane logic to get everything wrong. One year he was arranging a trip to England and the travel agent asked him if he would be taking his car.

"Ach man, you must be joking: of course not. Don't

you know they drive on the left-hand side of the road there?"

The travel agent was puzzled. "What's wrong with that?" he asked.

"I'll tell you what's wrong with it," said Van Der Merwe. "I thought I'd try it out, so on Sunday I drove from Johannesburg to Durban on the left-hand side, and believe me, man, it was bloody dangerous!"

Kingsley Amis

EAMONN ANDREWS

Let me tell you a true story about a musical instrument. It concerns a certain rock star, whom, for the purpose of this meeting we'll call Terry, a BBC Television theatre, a sound engineer and me. The sound engineer and myself had, for many months, been having fairly friendly battles about whether the sound was right for this or for that, and he always ended up by blinding me with science and decibels and electric circuits and the Lord knows what else.

On this particular day, Terry was rehearsing and I stood at the back of the theatre, unable to hear his voice above the sound of his backing group and himself twanging away at his guitar. Once again, I complained to the sound engineer. He moved the backing group grudgingly a little further away from the centre microphone. We tried again. I whispered to the engineer that I still couldn't hear Terry.

"Look", he said, "I don't want to upset your star, but he's drowning his own voice by playing too loudly on his own guitar".

The pleasures of the audience come before the moods of any star, thought I bravely. I took Terry aside and,

with my courage ebbing, hinted that he might be playing his guitar just a shade too loud and so obscuring the wonders of his glorious voice.

"Waddja mean?" growled Terry in his best rock growl. "Waddja mean? I ain't playin' nuthin'. These strings are made of rubber!"

PIETRO ANNIGONI

In 1952 the landlord decided to sell the studio rented by me in Piazza San Croce, in Florence. I had had that studio for 9 years and I loved it, so I was very disappointed. It was an old studio in an ancient palace, and the few cracks in the walls gave me inspiration.

Several cracks, I thought, would make the sale difficult and I started to paint the cracks very much in the style of *trompe l'oeil*, especially the one sinister crack of terrific realism coming straight down from the ceiling centrally on top of one of the windows.

The result was above my hopes. For 18 months many buyers left very reluctantly indeed. I think if ever I made a masterpiece I did it as a cracks painter.

Pich Annigoni

SIR FREDERICK ASHTON

The ballerina, Natalia Makarova, claimed:
"I have been loved by many men, but unfortunately none of them have been choreographers".

Frederick Ashton

ARTHUR ASKEY

All the jokes (the really funny ones) you read in this book will have been stolen from me!

So I am left with the story of the Irish priest who was terribly mixed-up – went to see a psychiatrist who told him to forget his Parish and his flock – go to London and enjoy himself for a few days. "Take your dog-collar off – and let your hair down" he said.

The priest did just that – went to London ... took off his dog collar ... saw a movie ... had a good meal and a drop of the hard stuff. Later that night, he found himself in Soho – in one of the 'clip-joints'. He sat down at a table and a topless waitress came up and murmured: "What

would you like to drink, Father?" He panicked – thought he must have left his collar on – and stuttered "How did you know I was a priest?"

"Oh! – I'm Sister Theresa – I go to the same *psychiachrist!*".

SIR RICHARD ATTENBOROUGH

It happened during the filming of *Dunkirk*. I had a rare day off, and my wife had driven down to join me in Rye. We were window-shopping for furniture when I saw this woman. She kept darting little glances at me and then looking away again. As we turned to another window, I could see her reflection. The quick glances had become a fixed stare. My heart sank to my boots. Why can't they leave me in peace, I thought. I don't want to sign autographs or exchange pleasantries with strangers. Not today.

Then my innate and over-weaning narcissism rose to the surface. After all, I told myself, I am a servant of the public. If this charming lady is trying to pluck up courage to tell me how much she enjoyed my last film, why should I deny her that small pleasure?

I turned to face her – all eyes and teeth – and said in my most dulcet tone, "Good afternoon". "Good afternoon', she responded. "It is Mr. Attenborough, isn't it?" I assured her that indeed it was. "Do you know", she murmured, "I nearly didn't recognise you without your monkey"!

PROFESSOR CHRISTIAAN BARNARD

During the period after the first heart transplant when I was very busy and had to talk at many functions, I had a chauffeur by the name of Van Der Merwe. He was enormously proud of his job and dressed very properly in a white cap and coat. During every talk that I gave he used to sit at the back of the hall and listen. One day I was very tired. He had heard me speak so often that he offered to give the talk for me on this particular occasion, so we exchanged clothes and I sat at the back of the hall in his white cap and coat and he took the platform wearing my Italian suit.

It then came to question time and Michael de Bakey, a famous American surgeon, who was in the audience, thought he would be very clever and ask a very difficult question about rejection problems. I could see my chauffeur was having difficulty, but to my surprise he turned to Michael de Bakey and said, "Dr. de Bakey, I am very surprised that a man with your qualifications and experience should ask such a stupid question, and to show just how stupid it is, I will ask my chauffeur who is sitting at the back of the hall to answer it for you".

HAROLD BERENS

Psychiatrist to patient, after three visits:

"I've got *bad* news and *good* news for you. The *bad* news is that I've come to the conclusion that you are a homosexual – and the *good* news is that I'm in love with you."

Doctor on telephone: "Mrs. Cohen, I must tell you that your cheque has come back."

Mrs. Cohen: "I know, and so has my *arthritis*.

       ★   ★   ★

Woman to doctor: "I want a little wart removed."

Doctor: "You're in the wrong office, Madam, the divorce lawyer is next door."

Harold Berens

SIR JOHN BETJEMAN

The poet Tennyson told his grandson, Charles, about a Russian nobleman who spoke very good English and who once came to stay in Surrey. He appeared at breakfast with a gun under his arm and declared "I have just shot two peasants!" His hosts started to correct him: "You don't mean peasants. You mean pheasants". "No" he contradicted them. "They were insolent so I shot them!"

STANLEY BLACK

The members of a synagogue congregation were shocked when they heard that their 75-year-old Rabbi was contemplating marriage with a teenage girl, and a spokesman was elected to see the old man in the hope of persuading him to change his mind.

The spokesman put forward all the obvious reasons against such a union – the unfortunate image it would

project; the erosion of the Rabbi's dignity; the embarrassment of the congregation, and so forth – but without
drawing any response or reaction.

In desperation, the emissary played what he fondly
considered to be his trump card: "Rabbi, apart from
everything else, there is also the medical aspect –
marriage between a man of your years and an 18-year-old
girl could be *dangerous*, and in some such cases death has
been known to ensue." There was the vaguest suggestion
of a twinkle in the old man's eyes as he replied, "My son,
that is in the hands of the Almighty – if she dies, she
dies."

JOHN BLUTHAL

Mr. and Mrs. Goldfish, only married recently, were already quarrelling. Yesterday's argument "What kind of a goldfish did I marry? You call this goldfish bowl a home?"

Today's argument: Religion.

Mr. G: There's a God.

Mrs. G: There *isn't* a God.

Mr. G: There *is* a God.

There *isn't*. There *is*. There *isn't* . . . etc.

"All right, smart Alec. If there isn't a God, who changes the water?"

*   *   *

True story: Australia.

Drunk near Central Railway approached me. "G'day mate. I'm an old digger; can you lend us a deener (shilling) to get to Bondi?"

(I was in a good mood as I had that morning received a tax rebate of £40.) I gave the drunk two shillings.

Drunk: "Good on yer sport, you're a real Christian."

I replied "No I'm not, I'm a Jew."

Drunk (waving a fist at me) "No you're not. You're a *real Christian*."

REGINALD BOSANQUET

An elephant and a kangaroo drive up to a bank. The elephant gets out with a brick in its trunk and smashes the bank window. The kangaroo goes hop, hop, hop in to the bank, holds up the cashier, puts the money in its pouch and returns hop, hop, hop back to the car, which the elephant drives away.

A police car screams up, grabs the nearest eye witness and yells "Did you see what happened?"

"Yes" says the eye witness.

"Can you describe the thieves?" asks the policeman.

"No" replies the eye witness.

"Why not?" demands the policeman.

"Because they had stockings over their faces."

Reginald Bosanquet

MAX BOYCE

When I visited Madam Tussauds in London, a few years ago, I was amazed to see large, life-size wax-models of the Welsh Rugby team being loaded into a freightliner container marked "URGENT For the attention of the English Selectors, Twickenham".

I enquired what they intended doing with them, and

was told the English selectors had ordered them and were going to install them at Twickenham. The English team were then going to practice tackling and sidestepping them. Intrigued, I rang the chairman of the English selectors and asked him how the new training method was going.

"Not very well", he said, "Wales won 14-6!"

BERNARD BRADEN

A policeman in a busy city noticed a little boy with a small case walking round and round the same block. Finally he stopped him to find out if he was lost. The little boy said "No, I'm running away from home". The policeman asked "Then why do you keep walking round the same block?"

The little boy replied "because I'm not allowed to cross the street".

RICHARD BRIERS

Customer to Waiter in Restaurant:
"Waiter – what soup is this?"
"It's bean soup, sir".
"I don't care what it's *been* – I want to know what it *is!*"

Richard Briers

ART BUCHWALD

From the Washington Post, April 5, 1979

COUNTRYMEN, HAVE YOU HUGGED YOUR
PRESIDENT TODAY?

When President Carter flew back last weekend from his political trip to Wisconsin he was very depressed. "It didn't go very well, did it?" he said to Jerry Rafshoon, his administrative aide in charge of image-making.

"I thought it went very well," Rafshoon said. "The crowds were warm and the fund-raising was a big success."

"But nobody hugged me," Carter said.

"I didn't know you wanted to be hugged," Rafshoon said.

"Sadat always hugs me," Carter said "So does Begin. Why can't my own people hug me?"

"Midwesterners don't hug people, Mr. President. Only Middle East leaders do that."

"How do I know the Democrats in Wisconsin are really behind me if they don't hug me?"

"They're behind you, but you're President of the

United States. The people of Wisconsin would feel they were being too forward if they hugged you. It would be like a Welshman hugging the Queen of England."

"Well I think it's nice to be hugged by someone. I don't

think we would have gotten a peace treaty if Sadat, Begin and I hadn't hugged each other."

"I'm sorry, Mr. President. I didn't know you felt that way about it. If I had known, I would have had one of our advance people in Wisconsin find someone to hug you."

"It wouldn't have the same meaning if it was planned. When Sadat and Begin used to hug me they did it on impulse. They really wanted to hug me. If you had arranged it, it wouldn't have meant the same thing."

"Mr. President, there are thousands of people in Wisconsin who would give their eyeteeth to hug you. But they were afraid that if they tried it the Secret Service would clonk them over the head."

"I understand that. But the governor of Wisconsin could have hugged me when I got off the plane."

"He's a Republican, Mr. President. He could have gotten himself in a lot of trouble if he had been photographed hugging you."

"That didn't stop Sadat and Begin. They had a lot more to lose hugging me than the governor of Wisconsin. How does it look for my image if the governor of one of the most important states in the upcoming elections doesn't want to hug me?"

"We can't make a Republican Governor hug you, Mr. President. But rest assured that the next Democratic Governor who greets you will give you a big bear hug, or he won't get a federal nickel for his State."

"I don't want Jerry Brown to hug me," Carter said.

"Don't worry about that Mr. President. Brown won't even hug his own father."

"On the other hand," said Rafshoon, "if we could get Teddy Kennedy to hug you, it might stop all these rumours that he's after your job."

"That's good thinking, Jerry. How do we do it?"

"We could tell him that we'll support his health bill in exchange for a hug on the White House lawn."

"Who is meeting us at Andrews Air Force Base when we land?" the president wanted to know.

"Vice President Fritz Mondale."

"What do you think, Jerry?"

"I don't believe he should hug you after you return from just a trip to Wisconsin. It will look too much like a put-up job."

ANTHONY BURGESS

Ludwig van Beethoven, eminent composer, had a manservant named Franz who had been faithful to his master for many years. But Franz eventually became disenchanted with Beethoven's way of life – the dirt, the

drunkenness, the bad temper, the irregularity with which he paid Franz's wages. So one day Franz said, "Herr von Beethoven, I am leaving you. Today. *Now*." Beethoven said "But, Franz, you cannot leave me. You have been my faithful servant for many many years. You have looked after me, cooked my breakfast, mended by broken pianos, found my ear trumpets when I have mislaid them, put me to bed when drunk and incapable." "Yes," said Franz, "and I am heartily sick of it all." "No, no, Franz," cried Beethoven, "You cannot do this to me. Why, apart from my faithful servant, you have been my inspiration." "Your inspiration?" retorted Franz. "Such nonsense. Your inspiration. Ach, you make me laugh –

Ha ha ha haaaaa!"

MAX BYGRAVES

A diner asks for lobster.
The waiter brings him a lobster minus one claw.
"Where's the other claw?"
The waiter, thinking very quickly, says:
"When they arrived this morning they were live and two of them started fighting. In the fight this one lost a claw".
The diner looks at the waiter and demands: "So bring me the winner"!

IAN CARMICHAEL

The ready and quick-witted response is, I suppose, a thing that we would all like to have permanently on the end of our tongue. I particularly admired one that Clement Freud produced during a TV quiz game on which we were both guest panellists.

"Who" the somewhat unctuous and nausiatingly patronising Question-master asked Mr Freud "is the person that you would most like to be stranded on a desert island with?"

"Practically anybody" replied Mr Freud blandly "who doesn't end a sentence with a preposition."

JASPER CARROTT

Seven or eight years ago, when I was still a semi-professional folk singer, I started an incredibly unsuccessful agency with some friends of mine. We decided to call it the Fingimijig Agency and the address was The Boggery Folk Club, Lugtrout Lane.

Each week, we had to advertise in the local paper. The advertisement would say "The Boggery Folk Club present Jasper Carrott and the Pigsty Hill Light Orchestra".

The first time I told the girl to send the invoice to the Agency, of course, she asked me to dictate the address. I did . . . The Boggery Folk Club, Lugtrout Lane, Olton.

In a broad Brummy accent she gasped: "Oh Kevin, you are *terrible* – you know you're not supposed to phone me at work" . . . and put the phone down!

BARBARA CARTLAND

The Army got a new Mini-Computer which went forward to Divisional Headquarters.

When the first test came it was used for a very special Divisonal exercise.

The Divisional Staff fed all the information about our

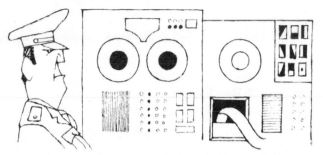

forces, and the enemy's, into the Computer.

Then the Divisional Commander said "Oh! Computer, what do I do? Do I stand and defend or attack?"

The Computer replied:

"Yes!"

Angered, the Commander asked:

"Yes, what?"

The Computer answered:

"Yes, *Sir!*"

FRANK CHACKSFIELD

One of my favourite conductor heroes was Sir Thomas Beecham or, as he was affectionately known to millions, Tommy. About to conduct a prominent but lazy orchestra one day, Tommy called for an "A" from the principal oboeist. This player had a wide vibrato and Tommy, looking round at the orchestra, said: "Gentlemen, take your pick."

Later, to the Cor Anglais who seemed to be asleep, Tommy said "Cor Anglais, kindly give some indication of your presence in this orchestra – that is if you are present – at 4 bars after letter G."

LESLIE CHARTERIS

Students enrolling at an American college were being subjected to one of those interminable, impertinent questionnaires intended to produce statistics on everything from their television watching to their favourite cereal. One of the questions was "Are you a virgin?" I have long been fascinated by the report that one girl's answer was: "Not yet!"

JACK CLAYTON

I recall Ben Hecht once telling me his favourite joke – which he attributed to Damon Runyon. I remember it because it is so short:

"Shut up!" my father explained.

JOHN CLEESE

What is red and green and does 5,000 RPM?
A frog in a blender.

HENRY COOPER

I was driving my car one day taking my manager, Jim Wicks, home after a lunch, and when I got to the top of his road I was following a man on a push-bike who was cycling against the wind and rain. So I thought I would have plenty of time to overtake him, and give him ample warning that I was going to stop.

As I pulled up he hit the back of the motor and over he went. He then picked himself up, came round the side of the car, and through the open window gave me a back-hander. Well, Jim Wicks jumped out (he was about 16 or 17 stone) and I got out (I'm 6ft 2″ and about 15 stone) and this guy was about 5 foot and 8 stone. He looked me

straight in the eye and said "You feel very brave just because there's two of you, don't you".

I was the British and Commonwealth Heavyweight Champion at the time. I think he would have done me in style if I had been on my own!

SAM COSTA

One or two things that have made *me* laugh . . .
Woody Allen said "I have this overwhelming desire to
return to the womb – any womb!"

*　　*　　*

Some Americans were drinking at an open air Café in
Tel Aviv, and at the next table was an old Jew – with
wide black hat, long sideboards and curls – and he was
crying bitterly over his "glass tea". The Americans were
very concerned, and one said to him: "Excuse me Sir, but
why are you crying like that?" The old man explained:
"I'm crying because I want to be with my people." The
American went on: "But Sir, you *are* with your people."
To which the old man shrugged: "No, I want to be with
my people in Miami".

*　　*　　*

The *shortest* joke in the world: Adam said to Eve:
"After we eat this apple we're gonna do *what?*"

*　　*　　*

Another American joke: Mother says to small son –
"Go down to the corner store and get 10 cents-worth of
cockroach powder, but don't tell them what we want it
for!"

Sam Costa

LESLIE CROWTHER

Magnus Magnussen on *Mastermind* asked an Irish contestant:

"Complete this line of a song – Old MacDonald had a . . .".

The Irishman replied "Farm".

"Correct" said Magnus. "Now spell the word *farm*."

The Irishman hesitated. "E I E I O".

Leslie Crowther

ANDREW CRUICKSHANK

In a time of drought in Scotland the Minister prayed: "Lord, if you could see it in thy boundless mercy to spare a few drops of rain for this thirsty parish".

At that there was a patter of rain on the roof of the Kirk. The Minister was heard to whisper through his breath "Lord, this is fair ridiculous."

Andrew Cruickshank

BARRY CRYER

A man driving down a country lane, ran over a cockerel.

He went to the farmhouse by the side of the road and knocked on the door.

When the lady answered it, he said:

"I appear to have killed your cockerel – I'd like to replace him."

"Please yourself – the hens are round the back."

LES DAWSON

An enthralled audience heard the celebrated explorer say: "I only had two bullets in my fowling piece and I fired one shot at the approaching tiger – but only wounded the beast. In panic I fled into a stone canyon and the beast crept up to the entrance – which was too small for it to get in – and waited for me to weaken and try to escape. I had one bullet left, but being an expert marksman I knew that if I fired the bullet at the stone wall 3ft away it would reach a velocity mach rate through a ricocheted trajectory gleaned from its parabolic flight – glance off a heap of Okapi Dung – go round the back of the tiger – enter its lumbar region and render the creature *hors-de-combat.*"

A little chap shouted:
"Did you kill the tiger?"
The explorer admitted:
"No – I missed the wall."

LORD DELFONT

Consulting a doctor about his health, a man was told – after examination – to cut out cigarettes, drink, meat and fish, and not indulge in sex, golf, sport or any other activity. The patient asked the medico if this would prolong his life.

"No", said the doctor, "but I guarantee it will certainly seem longer."

JACK DE MANIO

A few years ago, on the *Ten o'Clock* programme, I heard the following stimulating exchange:

Announcer: "Tonight's review is introduced by Norman Hunt."

Presenter: "No it isn't, it's Derek Cooper, but we won't quarrel about it."

       ★   ★   ★

Just after I joined the Overseas Service it was decided that the name Jack de Manio really wouldn't do, as it didn't sound English and people might think I was some sort of fake broadcasting from Turin. So I was ordered to choose a more English name. There was a girl I happened to be working with called June Marsh. Marsh seemed a simple, inoffensive sort of name, so I called myself John Marsh. The day came for me to try out the new name and it went as follows:

"Here is the news, introduced by June Marsh . . . No, John de Marsh . . . Oh hell, Jack de Manio."

That was the end of my new name!

JUDI DENCH

A famous actress, on hearing I was about to play Lady Macbeth – "Judi Dench playing Lady Macbeth? The letter scene will become the postcard scene!".

Judi Dench

GRAHAM DENE

A couple of funnies from my daily *Laugh Line*:

Two Irishmen were sitting in a four-engined plane flying back from a shopping trip to Paris when the captain's voice came over the speaker. "Ladies and gentlemen, one of the engines appears to have failed. There's

nothing to worry about, but we will be 15 minutes late in landing at Gatwick."

Five minutes later he said "Nothing to worry about, ladies and gentlemen, but one of the other engines has failed, and we will now be an hour late."

A moment later "er . . . sorry about this ladies and gentlemen, but the third engine has also given up the ghost and we will now be 2 hours later than expected."

One of the Irishmen tapped his friend on the shoulder. "Good heavens, Patrick do you realise that if the other engine fails, we'll be up here all night?"

*   *   *

In the bar at the United Nations, an American was boasting to his Russian and English colleagues.

"In Texas we had a guy lose an arm; we gave him a transplant and he was looking for work within a month."

"Comrade, that's nothing. In Russia, we gave a man a heart transplant and within a month, *he* was looking for work."

"I say, old chaps, that's hardly very impressive. We transplanted a whole person from Huddersfield to 10 Downing Street and within a week, half the country was looking for work."

ROBERT DOUGALL

When I appeared almost nightly on television my face, inevitably, became part of the national wallpaper.

Now that I have retired from the news, reactions are rather different.

The other day, I stopped for petrol and a charming girl was doing the honours at the pump. After a few moments, she swivelled round suddenly and said: "You're very familiar!"

And I hadn't moved a muscle.

Robert Dougall

DENHOLM ELLIOTT

The meek shall inherit the earth – er – if that's all right with the rest of you, of course.

Denholm M Elliott

RAY ELLINGTON

Ray Ellington's last will and testament.
I, Ray Ellington, being of sound mind and body, have spent it all.

ARTHUR ENGLISH

I started at the Windmill Theatre on March 16, 1949. My father didn't want me to appear there. He said I would see things there I shouldn't really see. He was correct. On my third day I saw my father sitting in the front row!

HAROLD EVANS

I don't know whether it's true or false, but it's good enough for me . . .
Elizabeth Taylor's latest husband said on his wedding night:
"I know what is expected of me, but I'm anxious whether I can make it interesting".

KENNY EVERETT

A chap goes to the doctor with terribly bad breath.

"Can you do anything for me, doc? I'm losing all my friends."

The doctor says cheerfully, "Never mind, lots of people have bad breath; it's nothing to worry about." The chap

breathes on the doctor, who falls back into the bookcase.

"Well Doc, anything you can do?"

"Yes" says the doctor, "Eat a pound of Camel dung."

"Will that cure it?" says the man.

"No" says the Doctor, "But it'll tone it down a lot".

GRACIE FIELDS

A fellow was in a pub – that was just about to close – and was chatting to the barmaid – when in rushed a young fellow who gasped:
"Give me a beer, quick."
He drank it and paid for it – then ran up the side of the wall – across the ceiling – down the other side, and out.
The other chap looked at the barmaid and said:
"That's a peculiar chap."
She answered: "Yes – he never said goodnight!"

Gracie Fields

CYRIL FLETCHER

THE ODD ODE OF SONIA SNELL

This is the tale of Sonia Snell
To whom an accident befell —
An accident which may well seem
Embarrassing in the extreme.
It happened, as it does to many,
That Sonia had to spend a penny.
She entered in with modest grace
The properly appointed place
Provided at the railway station,
And there she sat in meditation,
Unfortunately unacquainted
The woodwork had been newly painted
Which made poor Sonia realise
Her inability to rise.
And though she struggled, pulled and yelled
She found that she was firmly held.
She raised her voice in mournful shout
"Please someone come and help me out."
Her cries for help then quickly brought
A crowd of every kind and sort.
They stood around and feebly sniggered
And all they said was "I'll be jiggered."
"Gor blimey" said the ancient porter
"We ought to soak her off with water."
The Station Master and the staff
Were most perverse and did not laugh

But lugged at Sonia's hands and feet
And could not get her off the seat.
The carpenter arrived at last
And, finding Sonia still stuck fast,
Remarked "I know what I can do"
And neatly sawed the seat right through.
Sonia arose, only to find
A wooden halo on behind.
An ambulance came down the street
And bore her off, complete with seat
To take the wooden bustled gal
Off quickly to the hospital.
They hurried Sonia off inside
After a short but painful ride
And seizing her by heels and head
Laid her face down on the bed.
The doctors all came on parade
To render her immediate aid.
A surgeon said "Upon my word
Could anything be more absurd,
Have any of you, I implore,
Seen anything like this before?"
"Yes" said a student, unashamed,
"Frequently, but never framed."

BRYAN FORBES

In 1948 I had the great good fortune to be appearing in a new play by Daphne du Maurier called *September Tide*. The star was the illustrious Gertie Lawrence and her leading man was Michael Gough.

I had an arrangement with Michael Gough whereby I partly shared the services of his dresser, an engaging and eccentric character named Herbert. Herbert's principal responsibility came during the second act when Micky had to dive from the balcony of the house into the harbour to rescue the drifting boat. He dived, of course, into a pile of mattresses strategically placed off-stage and out of sight of the audience. He then had to plunge into a bath of lukewarm water to simulate the real thing for his reappearance. Herbert had to be standing by to assist.

During one matinée when the Aldwych was packed with middle-aged matrons all balancing tea trays on their knees, one of the cleats securing Michael Relph's weighty set suddenly gave way. The Stage Manager dashed in search of stage-hands to repair the damage before the set caved in. Now it so happened that this incident took place a few minutes before Micky was due to make his celebrated plunge into the harbour. Herbert was waiting

46

in the wings and, before he disappeared, the Stage Manager handed him a support rope and told him to hang on to it until help arrived. Meanwhile on-stage Gertie and Micky continued with the scene, unaware of the drama being enacted in the wings. Micky leapt from the balcony and groped his way in the semi-darkness to the bath of water.

During his absence Gertie went to a cupboard in the supposedly totally deserted house and took some towels out in readiness for Micky's drenched return. It was a vital plot point and carefully established in the dialogue that she and her son-in-law were isolated and alone – the storm was raging and there was nobody for miles around.

Unbeknown to Gertie, Herbert was standing holding the rope on the other side of the cupboard door. It was a hot afternoon and he was curiously dressed in pin-stripe trousers, collarless shirt and white tennis shoes. I should also add that he had a small Hitler moustache. The total effect was startling.

Gertie opened the cupboard door as she had done for the last two hundred performances and revealed Herbert. She was too dumbfounded to close the door again, and for

a few seconds she and Herbert stood transfixed like characters in a Disney cartoon. Herbert, being of the old school of theatrical dressers, was also a stickler for etiquette. He couldn't help himself. He gave a little bow and said "Good afternoon, Miss Lawrence."

Up to this point the audience had been mystified, but not unduly alarmed, by this sudden plot twist. After all, since they hadn't seen the play before, it was conceivable that Miss du Maurier had intended that her central character be suddenly confronted with Hitler in tennis shoes inside a cupboard.

But when Herbert paid his respects to Miss Lawrence the game was up. Gertie managed to close the door and then started to collapse. She turned away up-stage in a futile attempt to conceal her mounting hysteria and, of course, minus towels, bumped straight into the wet and unsuspecting Micky. He clambered back over the balcony and was greeted with a howl of laughter from the audience and a leading lady staggering around as though inexplicably drunk.

In such circumstances an actor's first instinct is to check his flies, which Micky did. Finding that everything was intact, he began his dialogue as per cue, but received no answering cue for, by now, Gertie – one of the world's great gigglers – was on the floor. Micky assumed that she had gone temporarily insane and carried on, giving her dialogue as well as his own, and attempting to retrieve the situation. Needing a towel, he went back to the cupboard. Renewed hysteria, this time in anticipation, from the audience. Micky opened the cupboard door. The cupboard was bare. And so the second act staggered to its conclusion, Micky having to wait until curtain-fall for an explanation.

Copyright Bryan Forbes Ltd., 1974, with the kind permission of Collins and Everest Books Ltd.

SIR CHARLES FORTE

One of my pet stories concerns an old couple in their nineties who went to see a famous solicitor in London to ask him to arrange for a divorce.

Thinking that it was very sad that two people who had been married for more than sixty years should be contemplating separation, the solicitor asked them why they were insisting on such a grave and dramatic step at their time of life.

The wife explained, "Oh we've been wanting to divorce for donkey's years, but we've been waiting for the children to die."

EDWARD FOX

A man in a village tobacconist shop asked: "I should like some tobacco for my pipe please; do you have any Three Nuns ready rubbed?"

To which the tobacconist proposed: "No, but I have got King Alfred in a tin".

Replied the man: "Have you indeed, then kindly let him out at once".

DICK FRANCIS

It is a well-known fact that many Irish, Roman Catholic priests are enthusiasts of horse racing, and the number of them who frequent the festival meetings held in this country has to be seen to be believed. Betting on horses is one of their first loves.

Well, just before the final race at the four-day Ascot

meeting, Father Murphy and Father O'Flanagan were seen deep in conversation at the side of the parade ring. And, standing quite close to them, was the race-commentator who was busily studying the colours of the jockeys just about to mount their horses. However, he overheard what the two priests were saying to each other:

Father Murphy – "Well Father O'Flanagan, I've had a terrible meeting, hardly backing a winner at all during all of the four days. Therefore I've got to back the winner of this race – the 'Getting-Out' Stakes. I don't know what my parishioners will say if I don't take something home."

Father O'Flanagan – "I too am in that position, Father

Murphy, and I'm equally anxious to back the winner of this meeting's last race."

Father Murphy — "Having a good look at the runners here, as well as studying their past form, I honestly think Lester Piggott will win this race. I'm therefore going to risk all my remainder on him."

Father O'Flanagan — "I'm of the same mind as you Father, and I too am going to wager my last bit of money on Lester. Before doing so, though, I'm going to offer a little prayer and trust the Almighty will answer it." So without more ado, off came his black hat, and he turned his eyes towards the heavens. "Holy Father, Heavenly Grace, may Lester Piggott win this race."

Whereupon Father Murphy pulled off his hat too. "I too am going to offer a little prayer and ask the Almighty for a little help." So he too turned his eyes towards the heavens. "Holy Father up in Heaven, and may his winner be 100 to 7."

The race commentator, who could hear all this, made his way up to the commentator's box. The horses 'came under starter's orders', closely followed by 'They're off', and the race commentator began:

"This is the voice of the Holy Ghost; Lester Piggott's been left at the post."

Dick Francis

LIZ FRASER

I've got a terrible memory. I forget every name I've ever come across and have insulted many people I've worked with by forgetting their names – and repeated the error to the same people over and over again.

I starred in a television play called *She* last year. We had rehearsed for two weeks and on the last days the "extras" came in (those who dress the scenes and never speak). I recognised one male extra from a show where he was again an extra from years back – and amazing! His name was Stephen, I recalled. So pleased at this feat I strolled across. "Hello Stephen, how are you?"

He paused (overwhelmed, I thought).

"I'm so sorry", he said, "I'm so bad at names – what's yours?"

Liz Fraser

JOHN FREEMAN

The following quotation from P. G. Wodehouse is the dedication to one of his books *The Heart of a Goof.*

TO

MY DAUGHTER

LEONORA

WITHOUT WHOSE NEVER-FAILING

SYMPATHY AND ENCOURAGEMENT

THIS BOOK

WOULD HAVE BEEN FINISHED

IN

HALF THE TIME

John Freeman

CHRISTOPHER FRY

During the rehearsal of a play the Musical Director had gone up on to the stage. The curtain was rung down without warning, and, stepping hurriedly out of the way he fell into the orchestra pit.

When I told my wife about the incident, after she had expressed concern about any danger he might have done to himself, she added:

"He hit the band that fed him."

Christopher Fry

54

SIR VIVIAN FUCHS

Culled from the classified advertisements of a small rural newspaper:

4 Sept.

FOR SALE: slightly used farm wench in good condition. A bit rusty, needs to be well oiled to work. 'Phone A. Scroggins, Hogsnorton 78.

11 Sept.

CORRECTION. Due to an unfortunate error, Mr. Scroggins' advertisement in the last issue was not clear. He has an excellent *Winch* for sale. We trust that this will put an end to the embarrassment caused to Mr. Scroggins and his housekeeper Mrs. Finch who loves with him.

18 Sept.

NOTICE. My W-I-N-C-H is not for sale. I've smashed it up. Don't bother to ring Hogsnorton 78. I've ripped out the 'phone. I am *not* living in sin with Mrs. Finch. Until I can get a new housekeeper she is carrying on with me.

A. Scroggins.

V. Fuchs

LLEW GARDNER

A true story . . .

During the Yom Kippur war I was on the Golan Heights with a film crew following an Israeli patrol advancing towards Damascus.

Suddenly we came under heavy fire from Syrian guns. We all took shelter in a captured Syrian bunker. I lay, a tin hat over my head, my mouth full of sand, pressed as close to the ground as possible. Suddenly I heard the voice of an Israeli captain in my ear.

"Wouldn't it be ironical," he said, "if you, a British reporter, should be killed here alongside an Israeli Jew whose parents came from Russia, with a Russian shell fired from a Russian gun by a Syrian soldier."

I took my head out of the dirt long enough to answer that yes, indeed it would be ironical, but would he mind if we had the rest of the philosophical discussion a bit later:

"I think they are firing at me."

He laughed. "Indeed they are," he said, "after all they know where their own bunkers are."

Shortly afterwards I made an excuse and left.

There are times when war should be left to the professionals.

56

SANDY GALL

It's really Groucho Marx's but I like it.
About Clubs: "I wouldn't want to belong to a club that would have me for a member."

CARL GILES

I quote from a past *Reader's Digest:*
"A notable exchange between an unpredictable and talented artist and his unpredictable and talented editor followed the late arrival of a cartoon.
The editor wired 'Brilliant, but unpunctual, unreliable, unbusinesslike!'
The artist, the famous cartoonist Giles, wired back: 'Dear Pot. Thank you for your telegram. Yours Kettle."

JOE GORMLEY

An anecdote which I use very often in my speeches as a Trade Union Leader, was a saying which I picked up from an old Miners' M.P., when he was fighting in the House of Commons for compensation for miners suffering from dust diseases.

He said, "Sympathy without relief is like mustard without beef". It illustrated his frustration with all types of government which expressed sympathy, but did very little else.

Joe Gormley

LORD GRADE

Somebody comes up to me and says: "What is two and two?" and I say: "Are you buying or selling?"

Grade.

JOYCE GRENFELL

One of my favourite 'over-heards' was said to a friend of mine, without any preliminaries, by her cleaning lady: "I don't like those chiffon nighties . . . they show your vest."

Joyce Grenfell

BILL GRUNDY

The Chairman of Daddy's company had accepted an invitation to dinner at home. He had expressed a wish that the children should be allowed to stay up for a while. Unfortunately, the Chairman had a positively enormous nose. Mother was on tenterhooks, impressing on the children that *on no account* were they to mention the nose.

He arrived and instantly the children were rivetted by his 'conk'. All through dinner they never took their eyes off it. Mother was unbearably screwed up with tension, but the children never mentioned it. They just stared. Finally the time came for them to go to bed. They did, with a last long look at the nose.

The door closed behind them and mother relaxed visibly, with a barely-suppressed sigh of relief. Serving the sweet, she turned to the Chairman with a huge smile and asked:

"And now, Mr. Stacpoole, will you have some custard with your nose?"

Bill Grundy

WILLIS HALL

Being a Yorkshire man and heavily into soccer, most of my funny stories tend to be about north-country soccer-maniacs. Perhaps the definitive one is about the Yorkshire fan who, after a life-time of supporting his local team, was rewarded with the prospect of a trip to Wembley, his favourites having fought their way into the final of the F.A. Cup. The fan managed to acquire a ticket for the game, journeyed down to London and joined the hundred-and-odd thousand lucky souls in England's premier stadium.

Fifteen minutes to kick-off and our lad was overawed by the occasion: flags, rattles, banners, scarves, and *Abide With Me*. Everything was wonderful. Save for one thing

– the seat next to his was empty. The following conversation between our fan and the middle-aged occupant of the seat beyond the empty one:

Yorkshire Fan: "It's unbelievable – an empty seat – at Wembley – on Cup Final day?".

Middle-aged Man: "As a matter of fact, that seat was reserved for my wife. Unhappily, she had the great misfortune to drop dead last Tuesday."

Yorkshire Fan: "I'm sorry I spoke, lad. You have my deepest sympathy. But, even so, surely you could have given the ticket away? There must be somebody in the family who could have found a use for it?"

Middle-aged Man: "Family? Family! Don't talk to me about my bloody family. There's not a sportsman among the lot. Every single one of them has gone to the funeral!".

DAVID HAMILTON

Presenting a *Radio Two* show can be great fun, and as a Disc Jockey one can get a kick out of discovering artistes who go on to become very successful.

I saw the Three Degrees at the London Palladium at their first appearance in this country, picked *Year of Decision* as my Record of the Week, and was delighted when it became a hit.

Their career went on to greater heights, but not everybody was acquainted with them when they got to No. 1 in the charts. A lady wrote in and requested me to play "When Will I See You Again" by that lovely girl singer Frieda Grieves!

There have been lots of gaffs on radio, but perhaps the best one was by a disc jockey who dedicated a record to everyone in hospital. The record he played was by McGuinness Flint *When I'm Dead and Gone.*

SUSAN HAMPSHIRE

When I was about nine, I was on holiday with my mother, who was a little deaf, and we were sitting in the late sun finishing our tea, when a waiter came on to the hotel verandah and asked my mother (who didn't drink) if she'd like a Rum Punch.

"Oh, Yes", she said, "I've not read it this month."

IRENE HANDL

A camp with a notoriously bad disciplinary record incurs wrath at the War Office.

An inspection is ordered by Top Brass. They are met by the Camp Commandant who claims that all is well, and that discipline is improving. He has orders to show them over the Camp, cook-house first stop.

A beetle-browed chap is peeling a mountain of spuds.

Top Brass greets him affably: "Good morning. What are you doing, my man?"

There's no reply. "Speak up!" barks the Commandant; "You're being spoken to!"

The beetle-browed chap shows a disenchanted eye. "'E can bloody see, can't 'e? I'm bashin' the bloody spuds."

"See what I mean, Sir?" the Commandant says happily; "A week ago he wouldn't have answered you!"

Irene Handl

SIR NORMAN HARTNELL

When I was setting out as a young designer, I was patronised by a domineering lady of vast proportions who brought in some old lace with which she wished me to trim her own black dress.

Grasping a length of the narrowest insertion of this hideous lace, I suggested "If we place this from your right shoulder to your left hip, it might help to cut your bust".

"Young man," she retorted, "I do not wish you to cut my bust. I thought this was a dressmaker's house, not a butcher's shop".

⋆   ⋆   ⋆

The Queen's dressmaker was lunching one day at a country house when a lull in the conversation left Sir Norman to compliment his hostess on a silver trophy in the centre of the table.

"I won it for one of my jumpers," the hostess explained.

"How clever," replied Hartnell. "Could you knit one for me?"

Norman Hartnell

MELVYN HAYES

When I was sixteen I answered an advertisement in *The Stage* which read:

BOY WANTED – SMALL – OVER 15

– FOR A TOUR OF WEST END MUSICAL

–MUST BE ABLE TO SING AND DANCE

– APPLY MISS TERRY OF TERRY'S JUVENILES

I was small, sixteen and unemployed. The tour was for *Dear Miss Phoebe*, following its successful run at the Phoenix Theatre.

I went to see the famous Miss Terry at her rehearsal rooms. She must have been nearly seventy at the time, but was leaping around like a child, surrounded by dozens of her "juveniles" (who I later discovered were mostly thirty-year-old midgets).

She asked me "Can you sing?" I said "No Miss Terry". "Can you dance?" I said "No Miss Terry". She looked at me, shrugged her shoulders, smiled, shrugged them again, sighed and said, "You're a nice Jewish boy – you've got the job . . . !"

PATRICIA HAYES

My daughter and I were in Spain with my grandson. The boy was about nine years old. One day at table, glancing through the phrase book in search of something to say to our charming waiter, I discovered the sentence "Is he a pansy?"

"Look," I said to my daughter, "What an extraordinary thing to find in a phrase book!" She laughed. My grandson demanded to know what the joke was. "It's a grown-up joke" she said, and closed the book. He snatched it up. "I'll soon find it" he laughed. He thumbed through the pages. "Got it!" he smiled. "What?" we asked. "It's General Franco's birthday!" he read out triumphantly.

There is a sequel to this family joke. Two years later we were watching a TV play, in which two women embraced rather tenderly. "A touch of General Franco's Birthday?" asked my grandson with a knowing smile.

Patricia Hayes

DICKIE HENDERSON

Sean Connery, Bruce Forsyth and myself turned up at the Royal Albert Hall, dismissed the taxi and entered the building looking forward to the Henry Cooper fight only to find that it was taking place at Wembley Stadium! Hailing another cab, Sean and I got in leaving Bruce to give the directions to the driver. As we drove off the driver said to Bruce "Don't I know your face; you're on the telly. What's your name?" He became rather persistent and Bruce was getting a little tetchy because if there is anything more worrying than being continuously recognised, it is not being recognised at all. So Bruce snapped "I'm Bruce Forsyth" and the driver laughed and said "If you're Bruce Forsyth, I'm James Bond". Sean tapped him on the shoulder and said "No, *I'm* James Bond."

Dickie Henderson

RACHAEL HEYHOE FLINT

A farmer's wife was expecting a baby and the town doctor was called out in the dead of night to the remote farm house, miles from anywhere, and without such modern attributes as electricity.

The doctor delivered the baby, and the nervous farmer was called to assist. He stood holding the oil lamp in order to give the doctor light. "Hold the lamp closer" said the doctor – and within minutes a boy was born; "Hang on a minute" said the doctor, "I think you are going to have twins – bring the lamp closer" and soon a twin baby girl came into the world. The farmer was still recovering from

the shock when the doctor cried "Hold on a minute, I do believe you are going to have triplets; come closer with the lamp." Lo and behold another baby boy appeared, to complete the triplets. The farmer sat slumped in a chair. "Good heavens", said the doctor. "I think it could be quads . . . come closer and hold the lamp. "Not blooming likely", said the farmer, "I'm not that stupid; it's the blasted light which keeps attracting them."

Rachael Heyhoe Flint.

BENNY HILL

A dozen or so Hell's Angels spent most of the evening in a roadside pub belittling a lone lorry driver. They poured beer over him, stole his food, insulted him and generally roughed him up. He just sat there and took it all, and then, near to tears he got up and left.

One Hell's Angel turned to the barman and said: "Not much of man is he?"

The barman looked out of the window, and said: "He's not much of a driver, either. He's just backed his lorry over twelve brand new motor bikes."

Benny Hill

JIMMY HILL

I remember only too well the day, as an ex-Fulham player, I returned to Craven Cottage to play with some of my middle-aged ex-colleagues, against the then Fulham first team for the George Cohen Testimonial Fund.

The old boys, giving away something like ten to fifteen years a man, began to perform surprisingly well and, to their own astonishment – as well as that of the crowd – took the lead. The Fulham lads began to get rather edgy realising that the boys of the old brigade were not going to relinquish their one goal advantage without a fight.

Suddenly Bobby Robson broke through on the right of the goal and shot fiercely against the goalkeeper's feet. The ball spun wickedly in the air in my direction at an angle about 15 yards from goal. I knew that I had to volley it. Only a coward would have shirked that responsibility, and there was no way I wanted to be accused of that. So, doing my best to ignore the fact that the chances of me hitting the goal must have been around 20-1, I closed my eyes and lashed at the ball. To my complete astonishment, it flew into the back of the net without the goalkeeper moving an inch. I had never volleyed a ball more sweetly in the twelve years of my professional career. Once the crowd had recovered its composure at this extraordinary happening, a long-suffering supporter was heard to remark in the stands, "It's a pity they didn't bloody-well play like that when they were here."

LORD HILL OF LUTON

Cockney kid – gazing through the window of a barber's shop while a customer was having his hair singed – cried: "Blimey, he's looking for 'em wiv a light"!

Hill, Luton

DAME WENDY HILLER

I was sitting in a tea-shop in Bond Street when a very determined lady leaned over me and said "Do you know, I thought you were Wendy Hiller! But now I see you are not. I am very sorry. Good-bye." Which left me with a kind of identity problem.

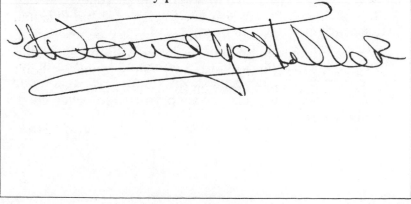

THORA HIRD

I was in hospital – in Lancashire – after a car accident. The result was anything but pretty; my face was blue, red, yellow and purple and half as wide again as it should normally be. I tell you these details so that you get the full picture. One afternoon a young lady was brought into the next bed to mine – prior to an operation to have her appendix removed.

Her aunt accompanied her. Plonking about four brown paper bags full of various fruits on the bedside cabinet, the aunt informed her neice "You'll not be able to eat these until after you've had it, because they won't let you, Mildred. And listen, love, there's no need to be frightened – 'cos it's nothing these days!" The neice assured her aunt that she was *not* frightened – but the aunt again told her there was no need to be, because it was nothing to be frightened about! The aunt prepared to leave and, as she passed my bed, she did a full "double take" and retraced her steps. Bending down – until her mouth was within a

couple of inches of my ear, she bawled, "Is it *Thora*???!" After nearly jumping out of my skin I feebly nodded.

"Eeeeeee . . ." she continued "what a sight . . . what a sample". Then, after straightening up and staring at me for a moment – she bent down to my ear again and bawled, "I say – what a good job you were never good-looking before!"

Thora Hird

VALERIE HOBSON

A Bishop and an Admiral who had disliked each other intensely for years, met at Victoria Station. Each was in full uniform and robes, having been to a garden party at the Palace.

The Bishop went up to the Admiral and said "Porter, is this the right platform for Dorking?" "Yes Madam" replied the Admiral, "But do you think it wise to be travelling in your condition?"

Valerie Hobson

WILLIAM DOUGLAS HOME

Lord Melbourne, the Whig Prime Minister, turned in the doorway, as he was leaving a Cabinet Meeting, and addressed his assembled colleagues:

"Gentlemen, did we say we would put a penny on the price of bread or take a penny off? It doesn't much matter which, but we'd better all say the same thing in the morning!"

GORDON HONEYCOMBE

Not so long ago, I went to Somerset to spend the weekend with friends – a young married couple who lived in a country cottage. On my arrival, tired and jaded after the journey, I asked if I might have a bath. "Help yourself", they said, casually – "The water's hot, there's a towel in the cupboard." So I went upstairs, ran the water and settled gratefully into the bath. To add to its luxury I borrowed some of the bath salts in a glass jar by the tap. "They won't mind", I thought. But the salts produced no bubbles and not much of a froth. A cheap variety, I concluded.

After the bath, I dressed and returned to the sitting-room, refreshed and glowing. "Everything all right?" they asked. "Yes", I said, and being an honest sort, owned up to using some of their bath salts. "What bath salts?" they demanded. "The ones in the jar", I replied – "Pale green."

At this they fell about, shrieking with laughter. I gazed at them, astonished.

"Those weren't bath salts," they cried – "That was bath *cleaning-powder!*"

All week-end they giggled and called me Flash Gordon.

Gordon Honeycombe

TREVOR HOWARD

'Twas an evening in November
As I very well remember
I was strolling down the street with drunken pride
But my knees were all a flutter
So I landed in the gutter
And a pig came up and lay down by my side
Yes I lay there in the gutter
Thinking thoughts I could not utter
When a colleen passing by did softly say
Ye can tell a man that boozes
By the company he chooses
At that the pig got up and walked away.

Trevor Howard

ROY HUDD

One of the quickest people with an 'ad lib' I've ever known was my manager of ten years, Michael Harvey.

A few year ago I did a spot on a star-studded TV show for the 50th anniversary of the R.A.F.

It was so star-studded, Hughie Green was the call boy!

One of the guest comperes was Richard Burton who was right in the middle of his second (or seventeenth) marriage with Elizabeth Taylor. Everything they did was front page news. As Burton was waiting, with Michael and I, to be presented to the Royals at the end of the show, he turned to Michael and said: "Is my wife here?"

Michael replied, from under hooded eyes, "I'm not sure. What does she look like?"

LORD HUNT

After the Everest expedition, Hillary and I were invited to come to SHAPE to tell the story. General Gruenther, by then Supreme Commander in succession to Eisenhower, was in London on official business and we were received at the door of the headquarters by the Deputy Supreme Commander in person. Monty gave us a smart salute, which Ed appeared to take as a matter of course in his delightfully breezy manner, while I did my best to conceal my own sense of the ridiculous in the situation as it applied to myself. I tried to put on an act of looking gracious and dignified, but I was feeling quite queer inside.

After the lecture, Monty addressed the assembled staff. "Well," he said, "you have now heard the story and I want you all to buy a copy of Hunt's book. Turn to Appendix III, and you will find the basis on which the whole operation was planned. Brigadier Hunt served as GSO 1 (Ops and Plans) on my staff at Fontainebleau before taking charge of the Everest expedition."

The inference was lost on no one – audience and lecturers alike: it was Monty who had planned the ascent of Everest. This was vintage Monty, if not in his finest hour, he was certainly at his typical and endearing best.

Extract reprinted from *Life is Meeting* published by Hodder and Stoughton.

RITA HUNTER

While I was rehearsing the Opera *Turandot* at the Welsh National Opera recently, we got to the place where Turandot (myself) asks the unknown Prince three questions. If he answers all three right he gets to marry her — if not, he gets his head chopped off!

After the second question the tenor was silent and the rehearsal ground to a halt amidst titters from the chorus. I didn't know why, until he eventually said "I'm sorry I can't answer — she's asked me the wrong question." — I had!

Roars of laughter and a red-faced Prima Donna — me!

Rita Hunter

TONY JACKLIN

A chap goes into a pub and the barman says "Good evening, sir, what is your pleasure?"

"Thank you very much, I'll have a scotch and a box of matches, please."

He then puts 5p on the counter and drinks the scotch. "What's the 5p for."

The fellow says: "It's for the matches, I didn't really

want a drink, but you asked me so nicely what my pleasure was."

The barman begins to get cross. "Sir, I was only being polite."

The chap is adament: "I'm sorry, but I refuse to pay."

He is barred from the pub.

Two weeks later he walks back in, and the barman shouts: "Hey you, out! I told you I never wanted to see you again."

The chap refuses. "You must have me mixed up with someone else. I've just come back after 4 months abroad."

After a close look the barman says: "I can't understand it; you must have a double."

"Thanks pal; and a box of matches as well, please."

Tony Jacklin

GREVILLE JANNER MP

The late Will Paling M.P. was attacking Winston Churchill.

"The Right Honorable Member is a dirty dog," he announced.

"Withdraw, withdraw," shouted angry Conservatives.

Churchill waved them down. "The honourable Member need not withdraw," he said. "Indeed, I would invite him to repeat what he has said, outside this chamber, and I will then show him what a dirty dog does to a paling!"

JIMMY JEWEL

My favourite anecdote is about my own family. We were a very close family. My sister shocked us all by leaving her husband and living with a man she was in a show with. He ran it and was pawning her jewellery to get himself out of financial trouble. My father and I went to sort this guy out.

They were playing a town called Biggleswade. We arrived at eleven o'clock at night, knocked up the night watchman at the Town Hall and asked if he knew where my sister was staying. It was over a shop in the High Street. We found it, and the landlady told us to go through the shop and take the door on the right at the top of the stairs.

As we climbed the stairs, I said to my Dad "I'm having no nonsense with this guy – if he gives me any trouble I'll belt him and you get my sister, put her in the car and I'll get the pawn tickets." We knocked on the door and went in. They were sitting in two arm chairs; I walked over to the guy and said "Is your name Raleano?" "Yes," he said. "Stand up," I commanded. He started to stand up, and he

never stopped. He was six-feet-seven-inches tall, and someone had forgotten to tell me he was a professional strong man that used to carry a grand piano on his back.

"Well, let's sit down and talk this over", I said.

Jimmy Jewel

BRIAN JOHNSTON

A woman went to see her doctor because she had a bad cough. He examined her and then asked:

"Do you ever get a tickle in the morning?"

"I used to", she replied, "But we've changed the milkman!"

PETER JONES

Everyone who's been on television has stories of the things fans say to them. My favourite was made by a woman who stopped me in the street:

"Oooh, Mr. Jones ... I love your new show – it's so mediocre, there's something in it for the whole family!"

MIRIAM KARLIN

Jewish father, very successful in business, wants to give his son the Bar-Mitzvah to end all Bar-Mitzvahs. After the Buffet Reception a fleet of cars takes the entire gathering of 200 people to Heathrow – a privately-chartered jumbo-jet takes them to Nairobi – and there

they mount astride a line of elephants. They then proceed on safari into the heart of the jungle. Suddenly, the procession of animals grinds to a halt. The father goes on ahead to see the reason. He comes back and calls to the party:

"I'm so sorry for the hold-up, my friends, but we have to wait for the Bar-Mitzvah coming the other way".

Miriam Karlin

BARBARA KELLY

A little girl came up to her mother excitedly with a carton of cereal, and said "Look Mummy, if you can say in 10 words why you would like a puppy, the person who says it best will win one!"

Her mother, busy in the kitchen, said "That's *all* we need." The little girl promptly went to her room, sat down, and filled in the coupon on the packet with the words "I would like a puppy because my Mummy says That's all we need", and sent it off.

She won.

LOUIS KENTNER

In the Rabbi's court, two litigants appear. One of them, Mr. Cohen, puts his case. The Rabbi strokes his beard and says: "Mr. Cohen, I think you are right." The other man, Mr. Bloom, outlines his case and the Rabbi once more strokes his beard: "Mr. Bloom, I think you are right."

Thereupon an irate member of the community rises:

"Rabbi, how can you be such a fool? If Mr. Cohen is right, then Mr. Bloom cannot be right. If Mr. Bloom is right, Mr. Cohen cannot be right."

"And you, Mr. Finkelstein", maintains the Rabbi – still stroking the beard – "You are right too."

ROGER KITTER

A man walks out of a house in Belfast.

Another man walks up to him and sticks a gun to his head saying, "Are you a Protestant or a Catholic?"

The first man, not knowing how to reply for fear of being shot if he says the wrong thing, thinks for a minute and finally answers, "As a matter of fact, I'm Jewish."

To which the gunman chuckles, "Boy, I must be the luckiest Arab in Belfast tonight."

Roger Kitter

ROBIN KNOX-JOHNSTON

While passing through the tropics on my single-handed, non-stop voyage around the world, the weather was extremely hot, so I did not bother to wear any clothing. I went below to make lunch and, once the stew was hot, took the pressure cooker off the stove and placed it on the bench at the aft end of the cabin. I turned round to put the kettle on the stove for coffee, and then sat down – on top of the pressure cooker!

DAVID KOSSOFF

The Rabbi and Sophie were giving supper to a favourite guest. Isaac the Beggar, who not only was good company, with wonderful stories of his wandering life, but who also had recently brought off a coup that had made the whole town laugh. It had begun at this very table, in Mark's house, a few weeks before. The supper talk had been of the little hospital in the town, which was always short of money. For a new stove, logs for burning, blankets, repairs, everything. There was no State aid; it was the town's business.

Isaac had pondered. "Long ago, Rabbi," he said, "about the time you first came here to Klaneshtetl, we had a doctor called Molka. He was born here and the town helped him to go away to University to become a doctor. He gave us a year or two and then went to Moscow where he is now a great man called Professor Molkonin."

"I remember him," said Sophie, who'd been born in the town. "Perhaps he would help the hospital. He worked there, he comes from Klaneshtetl, and he's Jewish."

"Not according to him," said Isaac. "Moscow born and bred and positively not Jewish. He is the head of a large teaching hospital. A famous lecturer and surgeon. His lecture theatre named after him. Very rich indeed. Friend of the Czar, who he treats for dandruff. I think I'll go and see him."

"The Czar?" said Mark, chuckling.

"Molkonin – Molka," said Isaac.

"For dandruff?" said Mark.

"For money," said Isaac. And was gone next day. Mark

did not give it too much thought. The Beggar often went off to far-off places. Famous. A leader of his profession.

Oddly, Mark heard the story first, not from Isaac, but in a letter from a friend in Moscow who worked at the Molkonin hospital.

The Beggar had presented himself, with fur cap, boots

and bundle, in the Great Man's waiting room. Who sent you? he was asked. Nobody. Appointment? No. Money? No. Quite impossible then. Then I'll wait.

He waited six days, in fur cap and muddy boots. From

the bundle, strong-smelling cheese and garlic sausage. Black village bread.

The Professor, they at last told him, uses in his lectures poor patients who are ill. You can join them. Tomorrow morning. Without clothes. Can I keep on the cap, and the boots? Very well.

Lecture theatre packed. Isaac at end of the line. Enter Molkonin, obviously held in great respect. Each patient shown, discussed and dismissed. Now it's Isaac's turn. In fur cap, boots and nothing else. Wiry, muscular, weather-beaten. Steady eyes.

"A new patient," said the Professor. "Not seen before. How can I help you, my friend?"

"You can help us both, my friend," said Isaac. "You can give me a large donation for the Klaneshtetl Hospital."

The Beggar helped himself to another piece of Sophie's plum-cake. "Not a bad fellow really," he said. "Examined me carefully, looked into my ears – at the same time telling me to keep my mouth shut – declared me healthy, put me up overnight and gave me my fare home and 10,000 roubles."

"For keeping your mouth shut?" said Mark.

"For Klaneshtetl Hospital," said Isaac.

from the *Rabbi Stories* published by Robson Books

David Cassoff

DAVID LANGDON

Professor Webster, the American lexicographer and compiler of the celebrated dictionary bearing his name, was once caught by his wife in the act of cuddling his secretary.

"Noah!" she exclaimed. "I am surprised!"

"No, dear." Webster replied. "I am surprised. *You* are astonished!"

MARGHANITA LASKI

The Clergy would have us believe them against our own Reason,

As the Woman would have had her Husband against his own Eyes,

What! will you believe your own Eyes before your own sweet Wife?

from John Selden's *Table Talk*, published 1686.

SUE LAWLEY

There is an apocryphal story that has been doing the rounds of BBC Current Affairs for some years now. Apparently it originally belonged to the first *Tonight* programme, and concerned a mouse that played the violin. More recently I have heard it in the context of a duck who was going to sing an aria from *Carmen* for *Nationwide*.

Whichever – the story goes like this: The owner of the amazing pet, who lived on a farm in the remotest part of Suffolk, rang the programme. A film unit, three lighting men, a reporter and a director were immediately despatched, but they had great difficulty in finding the farm. After travelling for many hours and making numerous enquiries they eventually found themselves on the right track. At last they saw the gates of the farm and with great delight they screeched into the farm-yard, whereupon they ran over the duck . . . or the mouse . . . or the pig . . . or the elephant . . .!

EVELYN LAYE

Some years ago, when I was playing with Dame Gladys Cooper in *Let's All Go Down The Strand*, a friend of mine went to a matinée and sat behind two old girls who, in the interval, decided to tear Gladys and myself to shreds. Gladys got if first; then they started on me.

"You know dear" said one old girl," that isn't *the* Evelyn Laye; that's her daughter."

"Oh really," said the other.

"Oh, yes" went on the first: "Evelyn Laye died of drink years ago."

Evelyn Laye

BENNY LEE

An old, Jewish grandfather, was sitting in his chair, drinking his glass of lemon-tea and watching his grandson playing on the rug in front of him. Suddenly he said to the little boy, "You know, Moisheleh, life is like a glass of lemon-tea." The child looked up and asked "Grandpa, why is life like a glass of lemon-tea?" The old man shrugged. "You're asking me? Am I a philosopher?"

*   *   *

On visiting a hospital recently, I saw a young man in bed – swathed in bandages – who had obviously had a nasty accident. I was told he was a member of the British bob-sleigh team. I asked him what had happened and he explained: "We met the Irish team coming up!"

*   *   *

A young Jewish Army recruit was singled out as 'officer potential' material. When asked by his Commanding Officer if he would like a commission, he replied, "No thanks; I'd rather have a straight salary!"

EARL OF LICHFIELD

Graffiti in London Airport . . .

An advertising poster read:
WITH BRITISH AIRWAYS YOU CAN HAVE YOUR BREAKFAST IN LONDON AND YOUR LUNCH IN NEW YORK

Someone had added:
AND YOUR LUGGAGE IN HONG KONG

MAUREEN LIPMAN

An old actor-manager, in the late 1890's, was financially embarrassed after a disastrous tour, and was forced to beg a lift back to London on a canal barge. "Honest Bargee" he declared from the shore – "Wilt thou take this noble player on your worthy vessel to London Town?"

"Aarright then" grumbled the bargee – "but you'll 'ave to travel with the cargo up the back there." The cargo, of course, was a huge pile of horse dung. But, having little choice in the matter, the impecunious thespian gamely climbed to the top of the pile, arranged his cloak about him – and the barge headed down the canal. At the first lock gates the man on the gate called to the boat driver, "Name Your Cargo" and the boat man replied (loud Somerset bellow) "Load of Dung and an Actor!"

The boat proceeded on its way with our hero looking more than a little perturbed until the next lock, where once again came the call "Name Your Cargo" – and once again soared the reply "Load of Dung and an Actor!"

As the third lock approached the worthy thespian leaned forward from his precarious position on the odorous pile and said "Before we reach the next gate, dear fellow – I wonder if we could have a little discussion about *billing*??"

Maureen Lipman

MOIRA LISTER

My first night in *Present Laughter* at the Haymarket, starring opposite Noel Coward, I was aged 22 – and petrified. The 'master' sent for me to go to his dressing room 10 minutes before curtain up. I thought it must be instant dismissal. Trembling I knocked on his door. An imperious "Come in".

He said "Now Moira – I have been very pleased with you and would like to make you a present for the opening night." Overcome I stammered "No no, please, it's such an honour to be working with you – I need nothing" etc. etc. etc.

He insisted, went to his dressing table, and took out a

2oz bottle of perfume called *Can Can.* (I still have the bottle). Handing it to me with a magnanimous gesture (it was half full) he said very grandly "That is for you. *I* have used the other half".

Moira Lister

SIR EMILE LITTLER

At a crowded dinner party:
"Can you hear me at the back of the room?"
Voice from the back:
"Yes, I can hear you perfectly, but I don't mind changing places with somebody who can't."

Emile Littler

LORD LONGFORD

About fifty years ago, when I was a young and fairly ambitious Conservative, I was taken for a walk during a country house party by Mr. Baldwin, then the Tory Prime Minister. At the time I was lecturing on political theory for the Workers' educational Association (following which I became a Socialist some years later).

Mr. Baldwin did not utter a word during the hour's walk. Finally I ventured to break the silence. "What political philosopher would you say, Mr. Prime Minister, has influenced you most?" Years later I realised that Mr. Baldwin was fundamentally disinterested in political philosophy. However he felt compelled to say something helpful: "I owe more to the works of Sir Henry Maine than anyone else." I persisted rather crudely: "What would you say was Sir Henry Maine's principal contribution?" Mr. Baldwin preserved an outward calm, but must have been considerably embarrassed. Eventually he replied: "Rousseau had seen the movement of the world history from status to contract. Sir Henry Maine discovered the real movement was from contract to status". There was a pause and then, with a charming smile of confederacy he looked at me. "Or was it", he said, "the other way round?"

Frank Longford

JOE LOSS

The Orchestra was playing aboard the QE2 on a world cruise. One of the ports of call was San Francisco. I had never been there before and, like all visitors, decided to do all the things that tourists do, including taking a ride on the famous cable cars. There was just one operator and, as passengers put their money into the coin-meter, he pulled a lever and a bell 'dinged' to record each person. My five companions and I climbed aboard; I put six coins in the machine and, with the driver's permission, pulled the handle six times; "ding, ding, ding, ding, ding, ding."

"You'd make a very good conductor," he said, and looked puzzled at the laughter that followed.

ARTHUR LOWE

In my TV series, *Bless Me Father*, I came across some amusing 'Irishisms' – my favourite . . .

Father Duddleswell, suspecting that his hospitalised curate, Father Boyd, is falling in love with his pretty nurse announces angrily:–

"I am going to pray that my heartstrong young curate keeps his head. Because if he doesn't, I'll knock if off for him!"

MAGNUS MAGNUSSON

If you'll pardon the bad language, my favourite anecdote is a conversation overheard on the bus from Aberdeen to Torry.

Aberdeenshire humour is mordant, pictish and devastating.

You'll have to bear with the dialect – but it's worth it!

"Hullo Maggie! Fit like?!"

"Nae bad, Beldie, This your quine?"

"Aye"

"Hoo ald is she?"

"Two".

"Ga'wa'! Kin she spik."

"Oh aye; Say something tae the wifie, Sonia."

"Awa' an' shite".

"Whatta rer spikker!"

LORD MANCROFT

When my father first stood for Parliament he was adopted for the Stretford Division of Manchester, which he fought twice without success.

He told Lord Rosebury, who had been his political guide, philosopher and friend.

"Oh", said Lord Rosebury, "You'll like Manchester; I know it well. I should like to die in Manchester. The transition between Manchester and death would be almost unnoticeable."

VIRGINIA McKENNA

Lady Penelope arrived back early from a busy day at *Thunderbirds*.

In the living room Parker poured himself a whisky, and was surprised by the Lady. Slowly she walked up to him and in a smooth, soft, gentle tone said: "Parker, take off my coat."

"Yes, milady" Parker replied.

"Parker, take off my shoes".

"Yes, milady".

"Parker, take off my skirt".

"Yes, milady".

"Parker, take off my blouse".

"Yes, milady" he said, still undisturbed.

"Parker, take off my bra".

"Yes, milady".

"And Parker, don't ever let me catch you wearing my clothes again."

LEO McKERN

The man in the hospital bed groaned and opened his eyes. His neighbour spoke:

"All right, mate?"

"Where am I?"

"Hospital. D'ye want the good news or the bad news first?"

"Gimme the bad news – it can't be worse than how I feel!"

"You were in a smash – they had to operate – they've taken both yer feet off".

"What!! Oh – Gawd!"

"Yeah, I understand . . . so d'ye want the good news?"

"You must be joking –"

"No – the bloke in the next bed wants to buy yer shoes."

Leo McKern

MICK McMANUS

Not all wrestlers are "all brawn and no brain". In fact, the majority are very intelligent; but there are one or

two a bit on the "thick" side.

I was once telling a joke in the dressing room, the question being –

"What is gross ignorance?"

And the answer –

"144 Irishmen".

One of the wrestlers couldn't see the joke, so I explained it in detail. He nodded his head a couple of times. He thought for a bit. Then he asked "But why 144"?

NORRIS McWHIRTER

Though she lived all her long life in the Highlands of Scotland, my great-great-grandmother had never in fact heard the bagpipes. About the time of her 90th birthday, the crofters decided they should invite a piper from Fort William to her tiny two-roomed house on Loch Eil. He duly arrived and gave the company his full repertoire of marches, schottisches and laments. As the last wailing note died away, her family gathered close to her box bunk to confirm that she had enjoyed this powerful performance.

In a weak but firm voice the old lady delivered her verdict – "Thank God there's nae smell".

GEORGE MELLY

Although it may well be apocryphal, my favourite story concerns Noel Coward who was staying with the Oliviers in Brighton. One Sunday morning, he went for a walk with their daughter, who happened to be his godchild, and was then about nine years old.

Along the front two dogs were mating.

"What are those doggies doing, Uncle Noel?" demanded the innocent child.

"Well dear," explained the master, crisply: "the one in front is blind, and his friend is pushing him towards St. Dunstan's."

YEHUDI MENUHIN

Trying to flag down a taxi in central London was far more difficult than I had imagined, when the cabbie learnt that my destination was Highgate Village. Driver after driver claimed that he was going off duty, having his lunch break, on his way to a funeral, short of fuel, and so on. I had almost given up when, at last, one caught my

eye and drew up. Once again I made my request, but this time it was met silently, with only a shake of the head and a shrug of the shoulders. Retreating from the open window, however, I was hailed by the driver's sudden shout of recognition. Eagerly I turned back.

"Hey," he said, "has anyone ever told you how much shorter you look off-stage?"

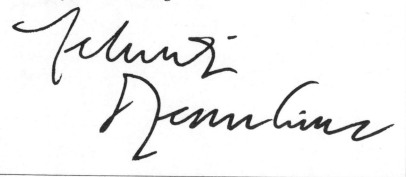

GEORGE MIKES

It happens in New York. A lady is travelling by bus in Brooklyn. It is half empty and she asks the driver:
"Driver, are you Jewish?"
There is a curt reply: "No."
Two stops later she asks again:
"Driver, are you Jewish?"
The driver is getting a little impatient.
"I've already told you, Lady, that I am not Jewish."
Another two stops later:
"Driver, you *are* Jewish, aren't you?"
The driver breaks down:
"O.K., I'm Jewish."
She scrutinizes him suspiciously.
"You don't *look* Jewish."

George Mikes

LORD MILES

During the processional hymn, a lady chorister caught the heel of her shoe in the iron grill covering the ventilation shaft running along the centre of the aisle.

Not wishing to hold up the procession she proceeded minus her shoe. A male chorister following close behind tried to pick it up, but it was fixed so fast in the grating that he couldn't retrieve it. So he picked up grating and shoe together, proceeding up the aisle with both. And the officiating bishop promptly fell into the hole.

Item culled from Ely Diocesan Magazine

SPIKE MILLIGAN

An archaeologist was digging in Israel, when he found a sarcophagus on which was written:

"Behold the first Jewish suicide".

He opened the sarcophagus. In it was a mummified Jew with a piece of papyrus clenched in his right hand. It read:

"A hundred to one Goliath."

BOB MONKHOUSE

A bar-tender takes £1 from a customer, puts 50p in the till, and the other 50p in his pocket. He takes another quid from a customer, again puts 50p in the till, and 50p in his pocket. Then he takes another quid and puts the whole pound in his pocket. The boss steps out of the shadows and says "What's the matter? Aren't we partners any more?"

Later, that same day . . . .

A man at the front door says: "Morning, missus, I've come to mend your doorbell." The woman: "I was expecting you yesterday." He replies: "I rang and got no answer."

But seriously . . . .

There's a bloke sitting in a public convenience when a piece of cardboard comes under the partition from the next cubicle with the message, "I'VE NO TOILET PAPER – HELP!" He pulls off half-a-dozen sheets, pushes them under the partition and somebody stands on his hand and steals his wristwatch!

And *those* are my favourite jokes!

Bob Monkhouse

LEE MONTAGUE

Benny was very well off – but not very good looking. A friend suggested that an eminent plastic surgeon in Switzerland could do wonders for him. So Benny spent some time in the care of the surgeon – having a little piece taken off here, a little piece put on there – a little on the chin – the upper lip extended. In short, a transformation. Benny returned to London and picked up his car at London Airport. While driving towards London, he was involved in a crash and found himself lying on the grass verge – dying.

Benny cried to the Lord,
"Why me, oh Lord, why me?"
And the Lord answered,
"I'm sorry, Benny, I didn't recognise you."

RON MOODY

A woman was granted a divorce on the grounds that her husband spoke to her only three times in the course of their marriage.

She was given the custody of the three children.

BOBBY MOORE

Paddy was trapped in a bog and seemed a gonner when Big Mick O'Rielly walked by.

"Help" Paddy shouted, "Oim sinking".

"Don't worry" assured Mick, "Oim the strongest man in Ireland and I'll pull you out."

Mick leaned over and grabbed Paddy's hand and

pulled and pulled to no avail. After two more unsuccessful attempts Mick said to Paddy, "Oim the strongest man in Ireland, and if I can't pull you out I'll have to get some help".

Just as Mick was about to leave, Paddy shouted "Mick, Mick, do you think it will help if I take my feet out of the stirrups."

PATRICK MOORE

The following story is, I understand, true!

A concert pianist was visiting Leningrad. He was fluent in Russian, and no lover of the general situation. Feeling somewhat wary of things, he looked round his hotel bedroom to see whether there were any hidden

microphones or anything else suspicious. He found some wires under the bed – so, using wire cutters, he severed them and went peacefully to sleep.

Next morning, the hotel chambermaid told him:

"Strange thing! Last night, for no reason at all, the chandelier in the dining room fell down!"

Patrick Moore

ROBERT MORLEY

I like the story of the man who came home one evening to find a gorilla loose in his garden. Keeping his cool and searching through 'Yellow Pages', he summoned a Gorilla Catcher. The man arrived with a dog, a net and

a gun. He explained the procedure, handed over the net and remarked that he was on his way up to climb the tree to agitate the branches, whereupon the gorilla would hopefully fall down and the dog would tackle the brute, as he was trained to go to the most sensitive part of the gorilla's anatomy. After that it was just simply a matter of slipping the net over the captured gorilla.

Half-way up the tree the catcher paused and then climbed down. "I forgot to explain about the gun; you keep that, and if by any chance *I* fall out of the tree . . . kindly shoot the dog!"

SHERIDAN MORLEY

Some years ago we had a cartoon in *Punch* (I fear I have never known who drew it; perhaps if he or she reads this book I might discover) showing a road leading into a new town.

On the pavement were three signposts, one behind the other.

The first said
HARLOW.
The second said
HARLOW.
The third said
WHO'S YOUR LADY FRIEND?

LIBBY MORRIS

I had always been self-conscious about the size of my hands. When I was young I thought they were huge; consequently, whenever I was fortunate enough to go out on a date, I would invariably try to avoid having the boy hold my hand for fear that it would be larger than his. But, one evening, I was fixed up with a blind date. We arranged to meet in the lobby of the hotel where I was engaged to appear in cabaret. At the appointed time, a tall, dark, handsome man approached me, and introduced himself. He was my date! I stood transfixed – open mouth, staring eyeballs, the lot. So much so, that I forgot my usual reflex of hiding my hand, and extended it. It became lost in his!

I thought I had big hands, but his were like baseball mits. I was overjoyed. As we stood there, shaking them, I said to myself, "This one isn't getting away" – and he didn't. He was Murray Kash. He became my husband.

STIRLING MOSS

A couple went to a West End restaurant and said to the waiter: "We only have £10; what do you suggest?" Replied the waiter: "Another restaurant."

A man went to the supermarket with his wife and tried to buy 5p's worth of potatoes. "I'm sorry," said the salesman: "we don't sell slices."

ARTHUR MULLARD

The teacher noticed that a pupil at the back of the class was not paying attention.

"Wake up, Jimmy!" he said sharply. "Tell me, who beat the Phillistines?"

Jimmy was startled and, after a long pause, tried:

"I'm sorry, Sir, I can't remember because I don't study non-League football."

RICHARD MURDOCH

I started my musical career when I was only three years old. We lived in a flat and there were terrible floods round our home that year. The water rose up and up until it reached our windows, and my mother saved herself by floating out of the window on the sofa.

What's that got to do with me being musical?

I accompanied her on the piano.

Richard Murdoch

DAME ANNA NEAGLE

During the filming of *Sixty Glorious Years*, the make-up that I was obliged to wear had to be seen to be believed. It was impossible to eat all day while I was on the set. So my late husband, Herbert Wilcox, who was the Director, advised me, the first lunchtime, to have a refreshing drink in the actor's restaurant.

I ordered what appeared to be just the thing . . . a long, fruity drink which I was able to manage through a straw.

It was *marvellous*. I had another. And then it hit me. It went straight to my head.

The sight of me tottering out of the restaurant, dressed as the ageing Queen Victoria, having unsuspectingly downed two very alcoholic Pimms, on an empty stomach, is something the rest of the cast teased me about for a very long time.

Anna Neagle

DENIS NORDEN

All the best jokes start "a man went into a chemist's shop" – so a man went into a chemist's shop and asked for a bottle of after-shave lotion.

The chemist asked: "Do you want it scented?"

Replied the customer:

"No, thanks, I'll take it with me."

TREVOR NUNN

Two Americans overheard in London:

"Hi, Chuck. How was your week-end at the Duke's?"

"Well, if the soup had been as warm as the wine, and the wine as old as the chicken, and the chicken as tender as the maid upstairs, and the maid upstairs as willing as the Duchess, it would have been a great week-end."

SALLY OPPENHEIM, MP

Victoria, my little grand-daughter, saw her mother getting dressed: "Mummy, why have you got such a fat tummy?" Her mother explained: "Because Daddy has given me another baby".

The little girl rushed in to talk to her father.

"Daddy, Daddy, is it true that you have given Mummy another baby?" "Well, er . . . er . . . yes dear I have". "Oh well", said the child: "she's eaten it."

Sally Oppenheim

DONALD PLEASENCE

During 1944 I found myself in a field in Northern France. It was a hot summer day, but not nearly as hot as the burning bomber out of which I had just jumped. A crumpled parachute was at my feet, and a dozen or so German soldiers surrounded me. At their head stood a young officer – straight and blond and proud.

In the Lancaster bomber I had just so wisely left, I was the radio operator. One of my jobs had been to see that the crew's microphones were in order. We had problems at high altitudes; the microphones would sometimes freeze up. To keep the moisture of the men's breath from the instruments I needed to cover them with rubber. I used to cut up male contraceptives, given away at the guard room. The top pockets of my battledress were always full of them.

The young officer marched over to me, his Luger at the ready. Expertly, he frisked me, and then plunged his hand

into my pocket – loaded with floppy rubber items. Hardly believing his eyes, he looked at his find and then stared for a long time into my face. I thought he was going to shoot me. He threw the offensive articles to the ground.

"You will not be needing zeese!" he said.

Donald Pleasence

MAGNUS PYKE

There is a succinct directness about epitaphs which, to my mind, can be very appealing. For example, Woolwich Churchyard provides the following gem:

SACRED TO THE MEMORY OF
MAJOR JAMES BRUSH
WHO WAS KILLED
BY THE ACCIDENTAL DISCHARGE OF A PISTOL
BY HIS ORDERLY
14TH APRIL 1831.
WELL DONE GOOD AND FAITHFUL SERVANT.

Magnus Pyke

STEVE RACE

In the *My Music* TV and radio programme, for which I act as chairman and question-setter, I once asked my panellists to give an impromptu suggestion as to what might make an appropriate registration number for a musician's car.

Denis Norden thought that Johann Strauss's car might have been registered 123 123;

and Vincent Youmans' car would of course be T 4 2.

John Amis suggested that a pianist specializing in Mozart Concertos might enjoy having a car with the number K.488.

For a fiddle player, Frank Muir suggested V 10 L I N

But Denis mystified us all by proposing a car number for Wagner, which he insisted should be 9 W.

"Why"? I asked obligingly. "It was the answer Wagner used to give", said Denis. "Whenever anyone said to him, 'Do you spell your name mit a V?' "

Steve Race

SIR ALF RAMSEY

"Be concerned about all life on earth – about the beauty and diversity of animals and plants – not forgetting that it's their world too."
By Sir Peter Scott.

CLAIRE RAYNER

I have a passion for appalling puns, especially the sort my twelve year old son brings home from school. Most of them are lewd in the extreme and, therefore, unrepeatable in respectable circles; but I quite like the riddle that goes "What succeeds?" The answer is "A toothless budgie."

BERYL REID

That lovely hot summer, I had several favourite friends to lunch—it was marvellous! We had delicious things to eat and a lot to drink.

After they had gone, I took all my clothes off and fell fast asleep on top of my bed. When I woke up, there was a note through my letter box. It said: "Your windows have been cleaned". I always look at my shoes a bit now when the window cleaner comes.

SIR GORDON RICHARDS

Let me tell you about two old friends of mine . . . Melbourn Inman and Tom Reece, the great billiard players. Inman thought he would like to own a racehorse so they went to Ireland to find one. Not only did they find; they brought one back.

The owner who had done the deal suggested: "Come inside and have a drink for luck." Inman, trying to be clever, stayed behind, put his hands in his pocket, pulled out a £5 note and gave it to the groom.

"Can you tell me anything about this horse," he asked.

"Yes, Sir – he has two faults. When you turn him loose in a field he's very difficult to catch."

"What's the other?" remarked Inman.

"Well, when you've caught him he's no bloody good."

Reece used to love telling this tale about his old rival.

CARDEW ROBINSON

A drunken gentleman on the way home from his revels happened to wander into a fair which had set up beside his road back. He staggered up to the stall which advertised "Three goes for 10d; Lovely Prizes" paid his money, took a rifle in his shaky grip and, to the astonishment of the stall owner, got 3 bulls' eyes. However, realising the man's condition, the owner thought he would be satisfied with something less grand than the tea service which stood on the shelves with the promise of "First Prize, Three Bulls-Eyes" underneath it. So he gave the man a live tortoise, and he staggered away with it quite happily.

To the stall owner's surprise, he was back again shortly afterwards and, demanding another try, repeated his feat. The astonished owner gave him another tortoise and away he tottered. He could scarcely believe his eyes when the man reappeared once again, and again he got three bulls. By now his sleeping conscience was finally aroused, and he gave the inebriated but deadly marksman the first prize – the handsome looking-tea service. The prize winner looked at it in disgust, blinked, shook his head and demanded:

"What's *this* rubbish! Haven't you got any more of those crusty meat pies!!"

Cardew Robinson.

DAME FLORA ROBSON

Both these stories are true . . .

When I was about 8 years old, I went to a morning school, and was taught by a doctor's daughter. There were some eight pupils, of different ages, the smallest learning from a book called *Reading Without Tears*.

One tiny boy who laboriously read out C A T, looked at the picture above, and said clearly, "Pussy" (actually, Puthy).

A year ago Brighton's team was taking part in an all-important football match. If they won, they would be promoted to the first division. The previous night the town was invaded by rival soccer fans, and they met in a bloody battle. Many spent the night in gaol or in hospital. On the Saturday morning I went to the Railway Station to meet a friend, and saw about 20 little boys (aged between 10 and 12) being marched in orderly pairs – one policeman in front and one at the rear. They were being sent home before the match. Out of the silence, came a bitter little voice:

"It's a shyme; (shame) we ain't done nuffinck yet."

Flora Robson

LEONARD ROSSITER

A theatrical story, but true, as it happened in front of my wife . . .

The scene: a repertory play some time back when there was the obligatory discussion between two people in dinner dress. In this case husband and wife were sitting on a settee (he in his hired suit) when he delivered the poignant line "Darling, what's gone wrong with our marriage?". Whereupon a moth flew out of his flies!

Leonard Rossiter

LEO ROSTEN

True story . . .

Years ago, when I first visited New York, an old Jewish *baubeh* (grandmother) stopped me and asked, *"Yinger mon"*, (young man) *"ir ret yiddish?"* (Do you speak Yiddish?)

"Fair", I answered.

Happy sigh:

"Nu, vat time is it?"

Leo Rosten

SIR STANLEY ROUS

At a local "derby" match in London, one spectator in particular spent the first twenty minutes yelling abuse at my refereeing. In his opinion I was blind, deaf, my parents had never married, and so on. When taking my position for a corner-kick I spotted him and said:

"I wish you'd shut up. You're spoiling the game with

your shouting. Who's refereeing – you or me?" Quick as a flash he came back:

"Neither of us!"

Stanley Rous

JIMMY SAVILLE

One of our ambulances went to collect a 'suspected overdose', on a Saturday night. The patient was a very friendly Irish gentleman.

"I took 120 tablets last night" he said.

"You mean tonight" replied the ambulance man.

"No" said the patient, "Friday night".

"Today is Saturday and if you took them on Friday you'd be dead now" explained the driver.

"Oh well" said the patient. "It must have been Thursday, then".

PAUL SCOFIELD

If you like graffiti . . .
I onced observed on Platform 10 at Clapham Junction, and on my way to the National Theatre, a huge religious poster bearing the legend . . .
THE WAGES OF SIN IS DEATH,
underneath which someone had written
YES, BUT THE *HOURS* ARE GOOD!

MICHAEL SEGAL

When I got married, my wife had a house and I had a house. We sold both to buy a cottage. But, not only did we have the contents of two houses – in mine we also had the accumulation of several generations of Passover crocks, enamel bowls, pails and plates.

We tried to pack everything in cardboard boxes. But the first elegant cupboard revealed a galvanised bath inside and in it, more Passover crocks. On opening subsequent glory holes, the baths got bigger and bigger. In the cupboard under the stairs was the biggest, brightest and rustiest tin bath of all. And altogether there were five. Moving Day was Thursday and this was Tuesday. Of course, there is a certain nostalgia attached to things of the past, but how do you convince your new wife that you need six tin baths of varying size in a tiny cottage? (Lucky for me she had none.)

The removers came. They did a grand job and cleared the house, but as soon as they drove away I realised I had forgotten the contents of the shed in the garden. In it yet another medium-sized tin bath. That made six. So I hired another van, and took the contents to the cottage. I travelled with it.

My wife was waiting at our new home for me to take her to an important appointment. Thinking I would kill two birds with one bath, I intended to stop en route to

deliver one bath to a cousin who had luckily expressed a desire to have it. Picture my wife, elegantly dressed, and me in my working clothes, hurrying from the cottage, clutching a huge bath. There was no car. Had it been stolen? No, I had in my preoccupation with the bath left my car at the old house.

The builder had a mini in which he kindly offered to take the tin bath, me and my wife to our destination. On to my cousin's. The bath was really a bit too big; did I have the next size down; don't leave it in the garden for my husband to see; he'll go mad; can you bury it? she said.

I was now without a car and at my wits' end. But suddenly came music to my ears . . . the bell of a Rag and Bone man. I threw the bath into his van — I swear he wasn't looking at the time. *One down and five to go.*

ALAN SIMPSON

Psychiatrist to Harold Steptoe:
"Tell me, as a child were you breast fed?"
"Well yeah . . . as it happens, I was. Well, we couldn't afford proper milk."

CYRIL SMITH, MP

When a new Member was taking his seat in the House I walked at the side of him, as one of his sponsors, and John Pardoe was at the other. The Member was a very small man and MPs were shouting "where is he then?"

This is typical of the humour of the House of Commons.

CHARLIE SMITHERS

How to tell a sex maniac:-

He suffers with three things . . . Firstly, a loss of memory . . . I can't remember the other two.

*   *   *

A drunk is walking through a cemetery at 2.30 in the morning. He hears tapping in the dark, and discovers a man with a hammer and chisel banging on a tombstone.

"You frightened the life out of me". He says. "What are you doing at 2.30 in the morning?"

The other whispers: "Bugger off: they've spelt my name wrong!"

LORD SOPER

The preacher had as his theme *Christian Perfection,* but he was anxious to point out that this was an ideal unattainable by such sinners as constituted his congregation. In the course of his sermon he challenged anyone

present to stand up and say he was perfect. To his astonishment a man in the third row did rise.

"Do you dare" challenged the preacher, "to claim that you are perfect?"

"No" said the man "I am standing in proxy for my wife's first husband."

BERNARD SPEAR

I was playing a matinée performance of *The Matchmaker* at Her Majesty's Theatre in the Haymarket, and decided to go to the Nosh Bar in Windmill Street for some of the 'best salt beef in London'. Usually I had a snack in my dressing room, but it was a lovely day and the walk would do me good, I thought – apart from the opportunity to study form outside the Windmill Theatre, where I had started my career back in 1943.

I sat down at my table, and opposite was a little old man who had obviously seen me on TV because, while I tucked in to an enormous plate of beef and cole slaw, he eyed both me and my food and said "Hullo Bernardel" (little Bernard). Now I weigh twelve stone, so you can see his eyesight wasn't so good! "What's the matter with you", he said, "you're on a diet or something?" I looked down at my meal. "With a plateful like this? You must be kidding." "Listen", he said, "I've been watching you. You 'ad no barley soup, and here they got soup like a king would be pleased to eat; also where are the chips? By me a plate beef with a salad, is a snack. So you're on a diet." Saying which he turned back to his lokshen pudding, which, had I eaten it, would have prevented my playing the evening performance.

While this was going on, the very tubby Jewish lady sitting in the corner had decided to attempt the whole menu, and was making a savage attack on a plate of roast

beef, baked potatoes, fried onions and beans. I swear there must have been a pound of beef on the plate. She struggled 'manfully' to the final mouthful, then leaned back against her chair, sighed and said, "Mr. Spear, I'm telling you when they say *sis schwehr zu sein a Yid* (It's hard to be a Jew) they don't know from their hand and feet what they're saying. Because I'm telling you, when you can eat a plate of beef like that ... to be a Jew is a real pleasure." And that is the simple philosophy which Hitler could never defeat.

DAVID STEEL, MP

I should like to offer this one, the origins of which I do not remember . . .

A telegram sent to Hollywood by a reporter read:

"How old Cary Grant?".

The reply came:

"Old Cary Grant fine – how you?"

JOHN SURTEES

True humour springs not more from the head than from the heart.

It is not contempt. Its essence is love. It issues not in laughter, but in smiles. Which lie far deeper. It is a sort of inverse sublimity, exalting as it were into our affections what is below us, which sublimity draws down into our affections what is above us.

Thomas Carlyle

ERIC SYKES

In my early days in television I was wearing a hearing aid during the filming of a TV show. Somehow I got crossed lines and all I could pick up on the contraption were the instructions for the camera crew.

"Tell that silly b___ to move across to the right", I heard.

Raising himself to his full height the silly b___ himself retorted in a tone as haughty as he could muster:

"I would rather be known as Mister Sykes!"

Eric Sykes.

SYDNEY TAFLER

It was Yom Kippur – the Day of Atonement – the most holy day in the Jewish Calendar. The day which Jews spend entirely in prayer and penitence, stopping for neither food nor drink, their minds occupied with nothing but communion with God.

The Rabbi left his home to walk – for riding is also forbidden – to the Synagogue. His route lay across the local golf course.

Now it so happened that, apart from being a most holy man, the Rabbi was also a fanatical golfer and, as he arrived at the thirteenth tee, an extraordinary sight met his eyes. A ball was sitting up invitingly on its small plastic plinth and by its side was a number five iron. It was just under two hundred yards from the tee to the green. Terror gripped the Rabbbi's heart. The temptation was irresistable. But it was the Day of Antonement . . . Evil to touch a golf-club, let alone play a ball with it.

He looked to the right and to the left. It was seven o'clock in the morning. There was no-one to be seen. In a moment of madness he picked up the club and swung at the ball. It was a perfect shot. The ball flew through the

air, hung for a thousandth of a second, and dropped with a plop on to the green. It rolled a couple of yards and sank into the hole!

The angels turned to God and looked at him with surprise. Then one, bolder than the rest, said: "You're a funny fellow. It's the Day of Atonement and you let the Rabbi hole out in one."

God looked at him and smiled.

"Who can he tell?" He said.

NORMAN THELWELL

The ability of human beings to communicate their most subtle thoughts through the spoken word is an endless wonder.

In the good old days when Liverpool still had beautiful tram cars rattling through its arteries, a little Chinaman was waiting at the tram stop at the Pier Head. He was

holding the hand of a tiny boy whose almond eyes glittered with excitement as a green giant swayed and clanged to a juddering halt. The child looked up at his daddy and said (as near as I can remember his words) "Ying yong, jing jong, ling long, ping pong". His father replied in a broad Liverpool accent:

"Yis, son, y'can ride on the top deck if y'like."

Fiendishly clever, these Scousers.

Norman Thelwell

LESLIE THOMAS

It was Easter and I was asking my seven year old son, Matthew, questions about the Crucifixion and the events surrounding it.

He answered correctly until I asked: "On the night before Good Friday Jesus and the disciples were gathered in an upstairs room for a very special meal. It was to be their last evening together. What was the famous meal?"

After some thought Matthew brightened:

"Soup . . . turkey . . . roast potatoes . . ."

TERRY-THOMAS

Here's a pet story of mine, about a chap leaving a country market, carrying two live geese.

He meets a girl and asks her which way she is going home – across the fields or by the road.

"Across the fields" she tells him.

"Alright, I'll go with you", he offers.

"Oh no you won't" she cries, "you might take advantage of me".

"How can I do anything to you with a live goose under each arm?"

"Well, I could hold them for you, couldn't I?" she explains.

JOHN TIMPSON

One of my favourite *Today* programme eccentrics was a man who collected dinosaurs' footprints – he toured the country looking for the fossilised remains of these footprints, and, when he found them, carved out the piece of rock in which the print appeared, took it home and put it in his back garden. He told us how a lady visited him one day, looked out of the back window at the lumps of rock all over his lawn, and asked,

"What are those?"

Very reasonably he replied,

"Those are dinosaurs' footprints." The lady looked at him in amazement.

"How extraordinary," she said, "that they should come so close to the house."

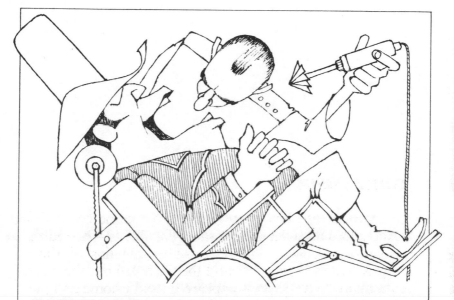

BARRY TOOK

A Texas oil millionaire had toothache. So he went to the dentist, and the dentist asked:

"Where does it hurt?"

The oil man replied:

"I feel lucky today – drill anywhere."

*   *   *

My favourite funny man is Woody Allen. His articles and films are so stuffed with funny lines:

On Beverly Hills: They don't throw away their garbage here, they turn it into TV Shows.

On Death: Death is one of the few things that can be done as easily lying down.

On Marriage: My wife thought I was a pervert because I drank the waterbed.

Barry Took

HARRY TOWB

Being Irish I like this one . . .

An Englishman walks into a country pub in the county of Galway. "I say", he says, "How quaint!. All this sawdust on the floor". "Ah, that's not sawdust, Sir" says the barman, "That's last night's furniture".

*   *   *

And my son, Daniel, told me this one:

"It's the middle of summer in the Antarctic. The baby polar bear walks up to his mother. "Are you sure I'm a baby polar bear?" She looks at him. "Of course you're a baby polar bear. Why do you ask?"

The baby polar bear looks up at her.

"I'm freezing", he says.

FRANKIE VAUGHAN

Two women met in a restaurant; the first woman noticed an *enormous* diamond on the other woman's hand.

1st woman: What an absolutely beautiful diamond.
2nd woman: Yes, it is lovely isn't it?
1st woman: I have never in my life seen a diamond as huge as that.
2nd woman: Well, it's known as the Plotnik diamond but unfortunately it carries a curse.
1st woman: Really – a curse – what is the curse?
2nd woman: Mr. Plotnik.

BOB DANVERS WALKER

Three forest animals were boasting among themselves which of them was the most feared.

Because of his ability to swoop upon his prey from above, the hawk claimed to be the most fearsome.

"Nonsense," said the lion, "every beast recognises my strength; none can challenge me."

The skunk then played his trump card claiming that he needed neither flight nor strength to strike terror in any creature.

At this point in the argument up came an enormous wild shaggy dog and swallowed them all up – hawk, lion and stinker.

Bob Danvers Walker

IAN WALLACE

A famous operatic bass went to sing the part of Mephistophles in "Faust" at a small theatre in the south of Ireland. He was very worried at the lack of scenery and effects, but noticed that the stage boasted a trap door such as is used by the demon king in pantomime to make his entrances and exits.

He decided to use it and arrived on the scene with a puff of smoke and a clap of thunder. Unfortunately there

came an exit when the trap door stuck halfway, and there was the poor old devil, visible from the waist upwards, trying like mad to disappear into the nether regions by jumping on the trap. At that moment a boy in the gallery shouted out:

"Hurrah boys! Hell's full!"

Ian Wallace

KEITH WATERHOUSE

And now, here are the results of the Sheepdog Trials.

All the sheepdogs were found not guilty.

[signature: Keith Waterhouse]

ARNOLD WESKER

The scene: after a banquet in a Jewish Country Club in up state New York.

Characters: The members, Jake Teitlebaum (centre stage) who's proposing for membership for the umpteenth time his friend Nat Zimmerman (off stage) who is always blackballed by the sinister Sontaag (craftily pretending he's asleep left on stage).

Teitlebaum: "To tell what a great human being Nat Zimmerman is I must use the entire English alphabet!

From A to Z I will tell you about this beautiful man." (Sweetly, not too loudly, in case Sontaag wakes up):

"A he is Admirable. B he is Beneficial. C he is Charming. D he is Delightful. E he is Educated. F he is Friendly. G he is Goodhearted. H he is a Helluva nice guy. I he's Inna-resting. J–" (Sontaag, eyes still closed, rises with the power of an old Biblical prophet).

Sontaag "J joost a minute!" (Powerful pause to open his eyes). "K he's a Kike! L he's Lummox! M he's a Moron! N he's a Nayfish! O he's an Ox! P he's a Prick! Q he's a Queer! R he's a Red! S he's a Shliemiel! T he's a Tochis! U you can have him! V ve don't want him! W X Y Z – I blackball the shmuck!"

[signature: Arnold Wesker]

MARY WHITEHOUSE

Travelling home from London one evening I shared the compartment with a woman who sat in the opposite corner. Every time I looked up from my paper she was

peering at me with a very puzzled expression, looking away quickly when I glanced in her direction.

It was just as the train pulled into the station and I stood up to leave that she suddenly burst out – "Oh *now* I know who you remind me of – Mary Whitehouse. But don't worry dear", she hastily added, "you're much better looking."

EMLYN WILLIAMS

Doctor Spooner (the most absent-minded don who ever graced the University of Oxford) met a friend in the High.

"Hello, can you come to breakfast on Friday? I'm having a few people in to meet my old friend, John Chetwynd. I'd like you to be there."

"But Doctor Spooner. I *am* John Chetwynd."

"Oh . . . Well, come just the same . . ."

Emlyn Williams

MICHAEL WINNER

Mrs. White gave birth to a baby which was just a head!

The doctor sympathised: "Never mind, someone will give birth to a body eventually, and we'll sew them together." So Mrs. White took the head home, called it Willie, and they lived quite happily.

When Willie White was eight, the doctor called again. "I've got very good news, Mrs. White. We've got a body and we can make a whole person for you." So Mrs. White said to Willie: "We've got something very special for you tomorrow. We're going back to the doctor, and he's going to give you a wonderful present." Willie looked up and groaned:

"Not another bloody hat!"

BERNIE WINTERS

Two Irishmen on an iceberg.
Paddy says to Murphy, "We're saved, we're saved."
Murphy: "How do you know that?"
Paddy: "Here comes the *Titanic*."

Bernie Winters

NORMAN WISDOM

The captain stood on the deck of his Roman galley and shouted to the master:

"Give me more speed!"

After a few minutes, when the ship did not appear to be going any faster, he called again:

"I asked for more speed. What's the matter?"

"It's that number twenty-seven," the galley master replied. "He just won't work and he's holding the others back."

"Well, you know what to do. Take the whip to him".

A little while later the master came back. "Number twenty-seven, sir." He reported. "I whipped him too hard and I'm afraid he's dead".

The captain thought for a moment. "Right. Whip the lot of 'em".

"What, everybody?" said the galley master.

"That's what you usually do when somebody dies, isn't it . . . have a whip round?"

Norman Wisdom

ERNIE WISE

Some people think that the most important thing in life is money.

It's not true.

Love is the most important thing in life.

Personally I'm very fortunate because *I love money!*

Ernie Wise

BILLY WRIGHT

As an England defender, I naturally never enjoyed goals being scored against me, but I had to marvel at that Hungarian maestro, Ferenc Puskas, when England met Hungary at Wembley in November, 1953.

Most soccer fans know they murdered us 6-3 that day, but one goal stands out for me. I can't remember how the move started – I can certainly recall how it finished. A long, low ball to the right of the England penalty reached Puskas. Wright came in for the intended tackle; Puskas stopped the ball with an unstoppable shot into the roof of the net past a helpless Merrick. The words of Geoffrey Green in *The Times* the next day summed it up "Wright, meanwhile, carried on for the intended tackle like a fire engine going to the wrong fire in a hurry."

Yes, it was one of the greatest goals scored against me.

JIMMY YOUNG

From *Famous Last Words*

General Sedgemore, during the American Civil War.
He ignored warnings against putting his head over the parapet to look at enemy dispositions saying:
"They couldn't hit an elephant at this dist . . . ."

David Jacobs'
BOOK OF
CELEBRITIES'
JOKES
& ANECDOTES

This book is dedicated with love
to Ruthie, Richard and Jonathan
—the kids who started it all.
E.G.